GHOSTIAN MANIFESTO

GHOSTIAN MANIFESTO

An Esoteric Christian Venture

BY SETHU IYER

Angelico Press

First published in the USA
by Angelico Press 2025
Copyright © by Sethu Iyer 2025

For information, address:
Angelico Press, Ltd.
169 Monitor St.
Brooklyn, NY 11222
www.angelicopress.com

ppr 979-8-89280-072-3
cloth 979-8-89280-073-0
ebook 979-8-89280-074-7

Book and cover design
by Michael Schrauzer

In memory of Jane Roll,
who said I'd write a book someday

TABLE OF CONTENTS

Perhaps this calling is the channel of invention
I will not blush if others see it as a crime
However dangerous the road, however distant
These things won't compromise the will of the design

Ten-thousand demons hammer down at every footstep
Ten-thousand angels rush the wind against my back
This church of mine may not be recognized by steeple
But that doesn't mean that I will walk without a God

Rolling river of truth, can you spare me a sip?
The holy fountain of youth has been reduced to a drip
But I've got this burning belief in salvation and love
This notion may be naive, but when push comes to shove

I will till this ground

~ Brandon Flowers, "Playing with Fire," *Flamingo*

I 🦁 CULT

SOULAR FLARE

Let us start this show off with a bang: after all, I hear that's how God does things, so why not follow suit? This work is about the reality of the soul and the advent of a renewed religious vision. We need not fear such words. A famous prophet once suggested that the revelation is ongoing, an open canon. The Old Testament was the Age of the Father, and the New Testament has been the Age of the Son; but now another door awaits to swivel on its hinges, revealing the silhouette of the Age of the Holy Ghost and the Everlasting Gospel.[1] We would all do well to remember that the Incarnation of Jesus was the inflection point of history's arc, not its conclusion; the nexus where things turned around, not where they were resolved. The end is not imminent until the Lamb breaks the seventh seal and unrolls the scroll of the final revelation.[2] Much work thus remains to be done — and, presumably, we are the ones to do it. The will of the Lord functions only with our cooperation, for He is the one god we can count on to not act like a fascist.[3]

---

[1] Joachim of Floris, in Frye, *On Religion*.
[2] Revelation 8:1.
[3] Berdyaev, *The Meaning of the Creative Act*.

I am stunned by the stupendous fact that the Star of David is identical with the ancient symbol for the heart chakra: such confluences surely suggest the presence of an alchemical heritage and a universal consciousness. David's psalms reflect actual *passion* for the deity, and the Ghost does indeed reside within the heart — not within the head, which is more of where the Devil tends to make his lounge. The twin interlocked triangles of the heart chakra's sigil, rising and falling, show the unity of spirit and flesh, sky and earth, God and man. The old tradition even knew that the color of the heart is radiant green. It is unfortunate that some heathen nations have claimed this hue (perhaps because they were in the desert, and green looked rather heavenly). In any event, let us embark upon a project to take back that verdant flag for the endeavor of the living soul, the guiding power of which is no one but the Ghost.

"There is a crack in everything — that's how the light gets in."[4] The original breach is deep within the human heart, and through that opening, the other realm manages to make itself known within the parameters of this one. Sometimes that chasm can expand, grow stable, become a channel of communion between the self and the deity; and through it may emerge a giant flare that could well produce a wholesale enchantment of our world. This is the genesis of prophecy.[5] Such things have been known to happen. Indeed, such things have always been the desideratum of spiritual development, ever since the start of our enigmatic species — and one of the greater

---

[4] Cohen, "Anthem," *The Future.*

[5] Heschel, *The Prophets.*

failures of these times is that people can think to do nothing but mock such a notion. In the absence of faith, only a living death awaits. We must aspire to become as lamps that have been plugged in, conduits of spirit's electric incarnation.

I propose that the adherents of this venture be called the cult of the Holy Ghost. (The more modern rendering is "Spirit," but the cadence of the old-school usage is intentional: the Ghost is spooky and haunts us still, and we are as haunted houses until we rest in Him.) When it comes to this project, the word "soul" is preferable to "spirit," because soul is incarnate spirit coupled with quickened flesh. Spirit in and of itself is as abstract as the angels — and in some important respects, the angels are lesser than we humans. Soul is spirit after descent, like God after the Incarnation. The English tongue needs more adjectives for soul. We should be able to speak of the heart generating soular energy, or the head being covered with soular panels.

Who could doubt that ours is an age of soular bankruptcy? For most intelligent men and women living today, the sense of impending civilizational decadence and doom is almost palpable.[6] Some inevitable airheads still insist that these are really the best of times — but that is only because they have no sense for soul.[7] They think that a quick glance at the GDP is all that's needed to convince ourselves that things aren't going to Hell. They fail to understand that reality is like an egg, with the soul for the yolk and the flesh for the shell. An egg that is hollowed out

[6] Barzun, *From Dawn to Decadence*.
[7] Pinker, *Enlightenment Now.*

may still look nice and shiny on the surface, but this belies how fragile it has become: one light tap of a finger would be enough to make the whole thing fall apart. And that, more or less, is where we are.

Innovation and restoration are two sides of the same coin, just as in the midst of the creative process, it is impossible to know whether we are inventing something new or discovering what has been there all along. One insightful man has this to say about the nature of poetry: "It is not satisfied with the idea of mere random tumble. It is *not* mere tumble, it insists. There is something here. There is something to be said. There is something, oddly, to be elicited from the tumble. Take it. Grasp it. Handle it. Try one thing and another. Try to shape it. Impose some form on it. Lo...lo...when you are finally satisfied that you have imposed the right form on it, you will wonder whether that form was imposed by you or whether it emerged from the thing itself."[8] God creates us, and then we manifest Him in turn. This project is a subjective vision of the great objective Subject, a fruit that also helps make real the Tree — and so on, paradox without end. There is nothing to do but to give it all our best and most honest shot.

DISORGANIZED RELIGION

"Spiritual but not religious" is a fashionable thing to say, these days — and it is easy to see why. Unfortunately, the organized religions often give so little in the way of genuine nourishment. Even setting aside the cases of clear abuse and corruption, religion

---

[8] Howard, *Chance or the Dance?*.

has too often become more of an identity marker than anything else: to be a Christian has come to mean little more than belonging to one particular cultural group or another, or pursuing some sort of political game, instead of seeking the Kingdom that isn't of this world.[9] Religion probably is important for consolidating entire societies — but this point is also very far from our locus of interest, and it has next to nothing to do with the seeker's passionate search for soular Truth. Jesus was an outcast, along with all the rest of the prophets, which may be a fact of some significance.

But we still have good reason to avoid calling ourselves "spiritual." That label sounds wishy-washy — too vague, as if we are unclear about what we believe in. The word *religion,* on the other hand, still resonates like a mallet on a marimba, conjuring the sense of a deeper commitment.[10] The word is thus worth keeping. Likewise, the historical Christian tradition can serve as a toolbox for building a regenerated vision, a treasure trove from which valuable jewels and minerals may be retrieved; but I want to put forth the conception of a cross-sectional cult, dwelling within the dimension of poetry rather than history, that also has Jesus as its fountainhead. Jesus will always be of paramount importance to us all because He is the Messiah, the fullest epiphany of the living soul, the nexus who connects our earthly realm to the final Heaven. Anyone with a deep concern for the soul thus eventually runs into Jesus, whether in this life

---

[9] John 18:36.
[10] Moonface, *Dreamland EP*; Paz, *Five Works*; Del Rey, "Religion," *Honeymoon.*

or the next. But this vision is still a little different from the historical Church, which has sadly often shown itself to be a nemesis of the living soul.

And that brings us to the cult of the Ghost. I have no desire to engage in an inglorious rearguard action to defend a past that probably falls somewhere on the spectrum between mediocre and miserable; let us instead work on something new and vital.[11] This is the kind of Jesus that we might have in mind, as He dwells within the olive orchard, talking with His Father on that final night: "I'd pray for this above all: that any church set up in your name should remain poor, and powerless, and modest. That it should wield no authority except that of love. That it should never cast anyone out. That it should own no property and make no laws. That it should not condemn, but only forgive. That it should not be like a palace with marble walls and polished floors, and guards standing at the door, but like a tree with its roots deep in the soil, that shelters every kind of bird and beast and gives blossom in the spring and shade in the hot sun and fruit in the season."[12] We see here Jesus, the paragon of a mad generosity; Jesus, the man who sought to take religion out from the synagogues and into the streets; Jesus, the greatest prophet of *disorganized religion*.

This statement will, of course, be suspected of her-esy, but that is part of the point: for ossified doctrine can misguide us, and to be alienated from a falsehood is to grow that much closer to the truth. At times our souls grow timid and suffer from a dearth of

---

[11] Frye, *On Religion.*
[12] Pullman, *The Good Man Jesus and the Scoundrel Christ.*

imagination, and we attempt to force the Light from Above onto the Procrustean beds of our own meager reason. Everything looks different when we begin to gain direct intuition of what manner of man Jesus must have been. Then the horrific chasm between the original and the counterfeits begins to come into greater focus. Then we are compelled to suspect that if Jesus returned to this fallen land today, many of the churches set up in His name would probably want nothing more than to kill Him again; for He remains as serious a threat to the powers of this world as He ever was, and the Pharisees and inquisitors are still in high places.[13] We are confronted with a vision of Jesus at Calvary, with almost everyone ecstatic with bloodlust; but He is looking straight at *us*, one by one, and asking us a single question: "Are you going to help them?" We must aspire to become the kind of people who could even begin to contend with that radical test.[14]

The organized religions surely aren't all a total wash — and that is exactly because countless brilliant soular folk have made their known or anonymous contributions to them over the course of the ages. Everything depends on the eyes with which we see tradition. We could speak of *soular tech* in this context, as well as a *pragmatism of the soul*. The Catholic rosary, for example, bears a striking resemblance to the Hindu mantra: a method to silence the mind, polish the inner mirror, commune with celestial powers. It sometimes does matter what specific soular tech is present (rosary beads are holy, ouija boards are

---

[13] Dostoevsky, *The Brothers Karamazov.*
[14] Miller, *The Crucible.*

demonic, and tarot cards are neutral); but in general, the mindset animating the use of such tech can be rather more important than the tech itself. Whatever brings the soul to life is good, and whatever kills it is evil: such is the doctrine that guides our project.

An overarching point here is that we humans will always evaluate things from our own specific perspectives and degrees of soular elevation. This goes for what we call holy books as well, none of which has an obvious or self-evident meaning that is accessible to all comers. There are folk who read the Bible and think that Jesus means to condemn some souls to eternal Hell; and in contrast, it is clear enough to others that such vindictiveness could never be associated with the living God — and that people who accept such a notion might be already inhabiting their own mental Hell.[15] Even the Devil can quote Scripture, as the old saying goes; but that is too often said in a self-righteous tone, by those among us who are somehow all too convinced that they aren't puppets possessed by the infernal ventriloquist. In short, vigilance is essential, but we must be brave in our advance all the same.

THE CHURCH OF MAGDALENE

We have ample reason to think that the Gospel of John has some connection with Mary Magdalene.[16] There is the textual evidence, for one thing. The famous "beloved disciple" emerges across the work; and for the most part the term makes sense, even if it often comes across as too shady by half. But the

---

[15] Hart, *That All Shall Be Saved*.
[16] Jusino, *Mary Magdalene: Author of the Fourth Gospel?*.

integrity of the text seems to degrade whenever Magdalene herself makes an appearance. She is present at the foot of the Cross, where she is supposed to be — but then the beloved disciple appears all of sudden, as if out of nowhere.[17] The same thing happens with the witness of the Resurrection: that is Magdalene's shining moment, but the beloved disciple has been painted into the scene again, and he is running to tell everyone the good news. The simplest explanation is that the text, at certain points, resembles a type of redaction job. We may sense that the name Magdalene was in the first manuscript and that, for whatever reason, her name was taken out and replaced with the "beloved disciple" wherever it showed up. But then that plan became unfeasible with the Cross and the Cave — maybe because tradition had already too firmly established that Magdalene was indeed present at those places? — so matters grew a little strange.

There is more as well. In the Gospel of John, a clear dynamic of rivalry is in play between Peter and the beloved disciple.[18] And this is very reminiscent of what is in fact reported in the writings of the Gnostics: it was well-known in that tradition that Magdalene was the disciple whom Jesus loved — and that Peter, veritable hothead, never quite got over the fact that he wasn't the favorite.[19] (And it probably didn't help to ease any tension that the preference went to a woman.) Overall, a lot comes into focus if we imagine that the beloved disciple is Magdalene, and that she is thus the source of the fourth gospel.

---

[17] John: 19:25.
[18] John 18:15-16.
[19] Barnstone & Meyer, *The Gnostic Bible.*

We may also observe that "John" is very mystical — much more so than the writers of the three synoptic accounts. We could thus perhaps imagine an early Christian sect associated with Magdalene, a band that first and foremost venerated her witness, before later veering a bit off course and morphing into the sorts of heretics who were expelled by the early Church.

Although I find this story very charming, I will concede that it could just be a flight of fancy; and in any event, my vision doesn't hinge on the contingencies of so eccentric a historical conjecture. It would be better for us to focus on the simple fact that Magdalene was the first witness to the Resurrection — which is well-established by tradition and even confirmed by the final evangelical edit. The Easter vision is all hers, and this point may be more crucial than we sometimes comprehend. The resurrected Jesus is the beating heart of the entire religion; and if He showed Himself first to Magdalene, then we can take that fact to mean that the Church of *vision* belongs to her. She is, after all, the apostle to the apostles, the original bearer of the good news that He is risen.

We could use the shorthand of *pChurch* to refer to the Church of Peter and *mChurch* to refer to the Church of Magdalene. pChurch is first of all about the Catholic institution, but it could also more broadly encompass all organized forms of Christianity as they have come down over the course of history. In contrast, mChurch is all about accessing the vision of that very first Easter morning. To see what Magdalene saw, and to know what Jesus knew: from our standpoint, that is the most important of all matters.[20]

---

[20] Urantia Foundation, *The Urantia Book*.

We might say that mChurch is the path of direct poetic apprehension rather than the mere "belief" of unconsidered dogmatism. This insight also suggests that mChurch is the home of the prophets, since to see what Magdalene saw would indeed make a man a prophet; and as such, it is the fulfillment of Moses's earnest wish that all of God's chosen would become prophets.[21]

That being said, an adherent of mChurch will probably find his best historical home in the midst of pChurch, given the world as it stands. The point here is simply that pChurch consists of exoteric structure — and as far as the living soul is concerned, adherence to that structure is only of secondary importance. In the same vein, we may suggest that the sacraments are accessed via soular power, and that the mere administration of their external forms by some mediocrity of a priest may not always be enough to render them effective.[22] Participation in pChurch could help people find their way to mChurch; but given the decadence of the institution nowadays (or has that just been more or less a problem since about the time of Constantine?), we have some reason to wonder whether this would be of much help for many men and women. To take a darkly germane example, it is only the exoteric pChurch that could ever have the problem of harboring sexual predators in its midst. Such a thing cannot happen with the esoteric mChurch, since when it comes to entrance into that temple of the soul, a turned heart is the original credential of admission.

---

[21] Numbers 11:29.
[22] Weil, *Waiting for God.*

The communion of pChurch provides an anchor in material history, which a man — most of all a poet or a dreamer — may badly need. But we must be careful to not thereby endorse a heinous structure of clerical power, or grant it undue legitimacy, or propagate the age-old falsehood that Jesus sought any dominion in this world. We shouldn't deny that Magdalene was His favorite; and while pChurch may be needed in this fallen dimension of history, we would do well to remember that we are still only making the best of a bad time while waiting around for the poetic Rapture.[23] To find the full Christian communion behind this veil of time and vale of suffering, we couldn't do much better than to return to where it all began: with Magdalene and her Easter vision.

ANONYMOUS ADHERENCE

"Not all who say My name will be saved," declared Jesus.[24] That makes sense enough, given that salvation is first and foremost a matter of an inner turning of the heart, a rising of the living soul. Any charlatan or hypocrite could recite a mere series of words for the sake of his own personal gain, and a deity who fell for such a gambit would not be worth believing in. But the Lord sees straight through us, and so of course not all who say the name will be saved, since the word itself is impotent if it isn't backed by sincerity and conviction. The other way around, however, must also be correct: many who *don't* say the name are surely saved as well. This point follows from the fact that the whole game has to do

---

[23] Fallon, "21 Days," *Sleepwalkers.*
[24] Matthew 7:21.

with the status of the heart, and not always a formal confession of faith that may or may not be uttered by any given person. If a man's heart is in the right place, then in principle it should matter little if he "officially" believes in Jesus — since his heart already does, irrespective of whether his tongue and mind decide to comply.

A certain discomfort is inherent in this suggestion, for it implies that people can believe in a thing without being aware of it; but everyday observation more than justifies such a notion. Most of us have at least two different cognitive systems going on in our minds at all times. There is our explicit ideology, which is what we formulate for conscious expression to ourselves and to the world; and then there is our implicit ethos, given subconscious expression via the real ways how we live.[25] Harmonizing those two systems is a difficult project that few would seem to undertake on their own initiative. For the most part, the systems sit next to each other in uneasy tension, trying to not strike up an awkward conversation. But just as a man can confess explicit faith while having an implicit heathen heart, he can also engage in explicit rejection of the faith even as he possesses the implicit heart of a believer. One thing we can be sure of in this world is that things like these are seldom what they seem. Who has the Ghost camped out in the tabernacle of his heart, and who does not? It all comes down to that burning point.

The concept of *anonymous adherence* has been floated by at least a couple theologians, although it can't help but conflict with more traditional notions

---

[25] Gramsci, *Prison Notebooks.*

of the Christian faith.[26] Such faith has long been thought to require explicit confession, which is supposed to follow from likewise explicit conversion, and then to find its expression in specific practices that have been approved by the community. From the standpoint of pChurch, then, the thought that people could believe in Jesus without knowing it would always have to remain a fringe phenomenon, insofar as the institution wishes to maintain its professed monopoly over the keys to the Kingdom.[27] The concept of mChurch, however, brings the riddle full circle. We may posit that the deep Church is the invisible one, extending beyond the bounds of any historical institution, and that its congregation consists of all the people in the world who have had a turning of the heart — which means that in order to evaluate membership, we must look at the heart and not the tongue.

Several reasons exist for why folk might not confess the faith they have, and likewise for why they may confess the faith they don't. I know countless people, for example, who aren't even able to think clearly about Jesus: for they were brought up in fundamentalist households where a narrow, vengeful notion of God was drilled into their heads, all the way back from when they were too young to even remember. As they grew older, they realized that they had been told a lie (and they were); and they thus turned against the faith of their early days. Since Jesus, in the cultural imagination, is rather wrapped up with pChurch, such people are then of course

---

[26] Rahner, *In Dialogue.*
[27] Shestov, *Potestas Clavium.*

uncomfortable with attempting the delicate alchemy required to extricate the hero from all the subsequent distortions. They may become good men and women; but as far as anything smelling of Christianity is concerned, they would just prefer to stay far away — and after what they've gone through, who could blame them? For my part, I had the good fortune of having been brought up in a different tradition, and I was thus able to encounter the Gospel as a very new thing, exactly as it was meant. What judgment could I possibly pass on others who weren't given the same opportunity?

When the paradigm of mChurch is equipped with the concept of anonymous adherence, the result is a powerful soular instrument that's capable of generating a vision of a radically universal religion. What matters is where our hearts are at; and we can never acquire full knowledge of another's heart, even as we can make some provisional assessments on the basis of the fruits produced.[28] We may affirm that not all "Christians" follow the trace of the Ghost, and that not all self-proclaimed heathens fail to do so. We thus see a flux and an uncertainty, as well as the implication of a humility regarding our judgments of others. We must worry first and foremost about our own souls and let the Ghost take care of His own mercurial work. The ideal would be overt confession coupled with a heart on fire, but we should be far beyond a petty insistence on it. The mysteries of the soul are worth so much more than what could ever be captured by tribal labels.

---

[28] Matthew 7:16.

AN ANCIENT ANIMOSITY

The priests and the prophets have never gotten along.[29] Part of it may just have to do with temperament: if they all took some sort of Jungian personality test, it is quite certain that the results would be poles apart for these two types of men. But the subtle animosity goes deeper than that. The prophet to the priest is as a vagrant to a cop: these figures just have different priorities and prerogatives, often irreconcilable with each other. The advance of one must mean the retreat of the relative nemesis, just as the progress of warmth implies the withdrawal of the chill. The priest is here to safeguard an established tradition and canon of knowledge: a role that, in the end, can't help but render him at least a bit authoritarian, despite his own best intentions. In contrast, the prophet is a conduit of new information, an ongoing revelation — and what he has to say likewise can't help but undermine the order and control that the priest seeks to impose.

Is it any wonder, then, that Jesus reserved his most virulent curses for the Pharisees, many of whom were the priests of the day? He called them whited sepulchers, bright on the outside but all dead within; He summoned woes upon them with a ferocity that takes us aback.[30] It would seem that the fulfillment of the prophets had no doubts about who His enemies were — and, alas, it is all too predictable that Caiaphas wanted to see Him dead. Thus was it always with the prophets.[31] Here is one rabbi's comment on the wild hearts across the ages: "The prophet is a man who feels

---

[29] Isaiah 11:11–14.
[30] Matthew 23:27.
[31] Matthew 23:37.

fiercely. God has thrust a burden upon his soul, and he is bowed and stunned at man's fierce greed. Frightful is the agony of man; no human voice can convey its full terror. Prophecy is the voice that God has lent to the silent agony, a voice to the plundered poor, to the profaned riches of the world. It is a form of living, a crossing point of God and man. God is raging in the prophet's words."[32] Such an intensity could only be seen as dangerous by the defenders of any status quo.

The calling of the prophet always comes from Above: he is haunted and hunted by the Lord, and his primary "choice" consists only of either accepting his destiny or else ending up like Jonah, stuck in the stomach of a gargantuan fish until he decides to reconsider his path.[33] No one but the Lord appoints a prophet as a prophet — and on that front, the prophet has an affinity with the poet, who generally appoints himself as one on the basis of bone-deep need and intuition.[34] This world cannot be trusted to produce such a judgment, since the world for the most part is hostile to creative imagination and wouldn't be able to tell a prophet apart from a madman if its own survival depended on it (which it often does). The prophet is anointed with the oil of invisible orders, a mandate from on high that only he can be trusted to render effective.

We are rather far here from the profession of the priest: go to the right schools, get the right training and degrees, and voila — a man is ready to become a priest, because the world tells him so. It is much the same method as how one becomes a lawyer or a

---

[32] Heschel, *The Prophets*.
[33] Jonah 1:17.
[34] Rank, *Art and Artist*.

doctor. Is there any reason to believe that a man who pursues such a road would necessarily have a special connection with the Lord? Or, given all the work that went into gaining social status, wouldn't a priest in all likelihood be susceptible to feel a divided loyalty at best, between the holy on the one hand and his institution (*not* intuition) on the other? And as time passes and logistical pressures mount, would the holy itself remain as anything more than a vague and distracting memory? . . . I suppose this assessment is a little harsh. Some priests surely could be holy men.[35] After all, mChurch is invisible, and part of the point is that its members could be found *anywhere*, even within the bowels of the pChurch establishment. The main hope would be that some men choose to become priests not in order to integrate into society, but rather to get as far away from it as possible. In that case, they may be less susceptible to an evisceration of soul.

The tension between the priests and the prophets perhaps goes all the way back to the figure of Moses — and indeed, we could see the conflict raging in his own heart. There is Moses of the Burning Bush, and then there's Moses of the stone tablets; Moses of the living water, and Moses of the dead earth; Moses the prophet, and Moses the priest. This ambiguity is reflected in the curious fact that God is said to have denied Moses access to the land of Israel. On the one hand, maybe this was because he had become too much of a priest and thus found himself unable to cross the magic threshold; but, on the other, maybe he was just too much of a prophet, and his own

---

[35] Tolstoy, "Father Sergius," *The Death of Ivan Ilyich and Other Stories*; Dostoevsky, *The Brothers Karamazov*; McDonagh, *Calvary*.

people had become a nation of priests — with Moses therefore being excluded from the start of that new and dubious venture.[36]

Everyone knows that we still have priests; fewer folk are aware that we also still have prophets. That mantle has largely passed onto the creative artists. Great art is meant to be *iconic*, in the sense of serving as windows into the Kingdom of Heaven. The Russians were probably the ones who had the greatest awareness of this fact, given that the title "Russian writer" has always been more similar to the designation "Hebrew prophet" than anything else — a keeper of destiny.[37] This concept seems to have faded almost into nothingness within contemporary America, where art under late capitalism has become little more than a matter of personal taste and cheap entertainment. The remnants of our culture are left to swing between nihilism on the one hand and fundamentalism on the other — twin enemies of the living soul. May this manifesto help restore the spirit of prophecy ascendant.

SAY ANNUNAKI

Legends speak about a race of hostile, other-dimensional entities who screw with us humans for their own benefit. It is said that they are reptilian in appearance, and they align with what the Apostle Paul called the Archons.[38] I will refer to them for now by another esoteric name: the Annunaki — my rationale being that the word rolls entertainingly off

---

[36] Frye, *Fearful Symmetry.*
[37] Morson, "How the Great Truth Dawned," *The New Criterion.*
[38] Ephesians 6:12.

the tongue. The Annunaki, however, are no laughing matter. They are false deities who, across the aeons, have managed to convince us humans that they are in fact true gods. They are incapable of generating their own energy, and their objective is thus to harvest our energy for their propagation.[39] In particular, they feed on vital life force, which is why they encourage strife all across the world: for they would prefer for a man to die when he still has young blood that they can absorb, as opposed to when his life has reached its natural end and has little left to offer in the way of nourishment. The Annunaki thus also spread the ideologies that make us humans believe that it is right and good to kill each other, cut each other down, waste ourselves unto oblivion.

Some say that the king of the Annunaki is Yal-dabaoth — a demiurgic figure who was responsible for producing this wounded world of suffering and death. Some also suggest that most of us have heard of him before and that we may call him "Yahweh" for short: which is to say, the main deity of the Old Testament.[40] We then see a pretender to the throne, who, characterized by narcissism, demands that we worship him. He imposes a false law that is marked by an unmistakable bloodlust, and he insists that those who worship any other god will be punished in the harshest terms (which itself is an acknowledgment that other gods do exist). Reading through books such as Leviticus, we find it hard to not at least sometimes suspect that Yahweh fits the bill: there are just too many reported instances of this figure calling for

---

[39] Wachowskis, *The Matrix*.
[40] Sigdell, *Was Yahweh an Anunnaku?*

violence and vengeance, and for very petty reasons that any decent man could only find to be reflective of an extravagant cruelty.

No real justification exists for this sort of thing — and if we find ourselves trying to excuse alleged acts that are beyond the pale, then perhaps the time has come to reconsider our stance. It is better to call the darkness out for what it is and preserve the integrity of human reason and moral instinct. We may well wonder aloud: why should we believe in an entity who is manifestly less merciful or virtuous than any common person with a heart? It is also from this standpoint that the modern project of deicide begins to seem at least a little compelling.[41] If the deity was in fact hostile to humans and wished ill on us for the sake of his own benefit, then human dignity could only be claimed via revolt against such a monstrosity.[42] Yahweh would then be the epiphany of phoniness, the truest conception of an utterly false god.

The one true Lord, of course, still lives, the same as ever. Our implication is only that a couple aspects of tradition may have misled us. From this standpoint, the deity whom Jesus called His Father was a new being introduced by Jesus Himself, never before fully known on the face of this fallen earth. Some support for this view can be found in Jesus's radical condemnation of the contemporary Hebrews: "If God were your Father, you would love Me, for I came from God and now I am here. I did not come on my own, but He sent Me. Why do you not understand what I say? It is because you cannot accept My word. You are from your

---

41 Pullman, *His Dark Materials*; Hashino, *Persona 5*.
42 Camus, *The Rebel*.

father the Devil, and you choose to do your father's desires."[43] What is Jesus really saying, here? It sounds very much like His point is that the perceived deity of the Hebrews is evil — and if that god is assumed to be the king of the Annunaki, then this train of thought would track. Jesus Himself would then turn out to be the true Lord who is here to liberate us from the arbitrary and delusional tyranny of the pretender.[44]

Such a perspective also introduces a somewhat dark resonance to an excessive fixation on the crucified Jesus: for this lines up all too well with the desire of the Annunaki for fresh hot blood. While we could never deny the salvific mystery of Calvary, that was also only one side of the coin; so it may be a good idea to dedicate more of our attention to the victory of Jesus over death, rather than any legalistic notion of a blood-price atonement. Here's a wondrous way to think of Him — the scene is the harrowing of Hell:

> They thought me rejected, destroyed. I wasn't.
> Hell saw me and was miserable.
> Death cast me up along with others.
> I have been gall and bitterness to death.
> I went down with it to the uttermost depth,
> and it released my feet and head,
> for it couldn't endure my face.[45]

And the trail He blazed is ours to take as well, as we walk on water with our vision fixed on Jesus risen from the dead. The story is ultimately not about some masochistic notion of human wretchedness and

---

[43] John 8:42–44.
[44] Shelley, "Prometheus Unbound", *Selected Poems and Prose*.
[45] Barnstone & Meyer, *The Gnostic Bible*.

sin, but rather about the true depths of our potentials, if we only managed to overcome the limiters that imprison our own holy powers. The Bridge to Heaven stands established, and now may be fulfilled the promise that we shall become as gods.[46] It only remains for us to find our courage and answer the call.

VEIL AGAINST VISION

A basic problem emerges when trying to consider the Bible as a unity; and it has to do with the fact that, if this is truly the case, then God too often comes off looking rather like a maniac. The issue goes beyond the notion of a "complex" personality, or a matter of God growing up over time (which would at any rate deny the concept of an unchanging deity).[47] Rather, the reader gets the distinct sense that multiple personalities are in play, each with their own divergent imperatives and goals. We find no honest way to square the God of the Gospel with the recurrent bloodlust found across so much of the Old Testament: not as long, anyway, as it is assumed that the singular voice of God is in fact recorded across all the pages of the Bible.

An alternative perspective does exist, however. The picture shifts into greater focus if we imagine that there dwelt a *veil*, or filter — sometimes more transparent, sometimes more opaque — between the words of the deity and the ancient Hebrews' perceptions of those words. Depending on where a man stood in relation to that veil, God could have looked very different. In fact, the spread could have been so wide

---

[46] John 10:34.
[47] Miles, *God: A Biography.*

as to encompass all of what must seem like an entire spectrum of schizoid variations. This is a reversal of perspective, through which the apparent madness is understood to be a function not of God Himself, but rather of the inconstancy with which we humans have seen Him across the ages. Some men may have witnessed God as if face to face and lived to tell the tale, whereas others glimpsed Him very darkly and also recorded their experiences. This dynamic could have been so extreme that some men even confused evil itself with divinity.

If *all* of these angles are recorded in the Bible, then what emerges is not a crazy deity who speaks to humans in many contradictory voices, but rather a single being who is heard via myriad different human ears. The Bible would then be the record of a continual struggle with the Lord: a picture that becomes clearer with every new prophet and turn of the cycle — and which achieves its epiphany with the Heavenly Father of the Gospel, presented to the world by Jesus. We thus observe an infernal veil that prevents the perceiver from understanding the truth about the Lord, intrudes between us and our direct grasp of His authentic voice.

Jesus was utterly original — but He still had His precursors, after all, and those men were the prophets.[48] A clear dialectic is present in the Old Testament where the people of Israel keep whoring after false idols time and time again, while the prophets likewise emerge to speak the true word and call on their people to repent, turn their hearts around.[49] There very

---

[48] Heschel, *The Prophets*.
[49] 2 Chronicles 7:14.

much seems to be a *religion of the prophets,* produced and regenerated by men who had some vision of the Heavenly Father — men for whom the veil became almost translucent, letting in the fullness of the Light from Above. We rest in sympathy with this inner tradition. The unity of the Bible may thus consist of its polyphonic presence, with its various books recording not the literal word of God per se, but rather the history of humankind's wrestling with the deity, including both purer and more corrupt elements, as the struggle wore on across the millennia. This amounts to reading the Bible in white rather than black — taking the same historical text, but applying a different hermeneutic lens.[50] The Bible would then, in fact, contain a summation and synthesis of human wisdom, in a very complex and paradoxical sense, with much of the Bible being the mixture between a divine voice and a muddled human perception of it: a confusion that is only fully abrogated in the final vision of Jesus Himself.

Likewise, tradition is correct to affirm that the Holy Ghost spoke through the prophets — although it often forgets to add that He continues to do so, and that the revelation is thus not over.[51] Some novels could possibly be worth more than entire books of the Bible, due to a greater density and accuracy of prophetic insight within those works.[52] A book might not be holy merely because it is collected in a historical compendium; and a book is not profane

---

[50] Blake, "The Everlasting Gospel," *Complete Writings;* Nietzsche, "On the Genealogy of Morals," *A Nietzsche Compendium.*
[51] The Nicene Creed.
[52] Dostoevsky, *Demons;* Vodolazkin, *Laurus.*

on the sole basis of its exclusion. What we need is an intuitive second sight, via the third eye, that is capable of the deep discernment by which alone we can come to recognize the cadence of prophecy when we hear it. Naturally, we are obliged to feel skeptical of the self-serving notion that pChurch and its tradition must be infallible because the Ghost guided not only the assembly of the Bible, but also all further historical twists and turns that set the meaning of the tradition and the text in stone.[53] Such fantasy hinders the living imagination, and this type of passivity could only generate at best a spectral faith lacking in vital engagement.

We thus tend toward the conclusion that the Old Testament is a rather mixed bag, in which a great amount of true and profound vision is jumbled up with what look to be grotesque blasphemies against the nature of the Lord. As such, we find that we must make like Moses and *draw water from the rock*.[54] What matters is not whether a man has read the Bible, but rather the eyes and ears with which his encounter with the book has taken place. To read the text, see nothing but rock, and then conclude that the religion of the rock must be ultimate truth — well, it would probably be better to not read the tome at all than to read it in that manner. We must instead find the religion of the living water, accessed via poetic vision and an embrace of a literalism of metaphor: for metaphor reveals reality, and our "literal" eyes are the ones that lie to us.

---

[53] Hart, *Tradition and Apocalypse.*
[54] Numbers 20:11; Morales, *The Divine Secret of Nothing.*

ASCENDING LIGHT'S HEIGHTS

So much depends on perspective, doesn't it? Two people can see the same thing, but they can see it in such radically different ways that each may well wonder whether the other is insane. Let us turn our attention to the following sketch:

R   B   R   B

X   —   —   X

In this diagram, R = red wall, B = blue wall, O = object, X = viewer position, and the arrow is the line of sight. Two scenarios are present here; the object stays in the same place across the both of them. But the person moves, and this fact will change the way he sees the object. In the first situation, the object will look like it is sitting in front of a blue background; whereas in the second, the person will see the object against a red canvas instead. It is the same object, and it hasn't moved, but the shift in perspective will make the viewing of the object a very different experience.

This is the gist of the concept of parallax: that even if two people see the same objective thing, their different standpoints can drastically affect their subjective encounters with that thing. Now, if we imagine red and blue to signify different *meanings* — say, red means rage and blue means sorrow — then the game becomes even more interesting. One person would see an angry object and another would see a sad object, even though the object is exactly the same in both cases. What we see depends on where we're standing.

We live in a time of intense ideological polarization. Events are continually taking place where half
the people in the nation think it's going to be the
end of the world, while the other half insist that it is
no big deal at all or even a wonderful thing.[55] Such
a situation is enough to make almost everyone feel
like they are losing their minds. We could say that
there is a huge parallax schism tearing the culture
apart, by which people have come to live in mutually
incomprehensible realities. Is an event a harbinger of
doom, or does it signify the rise of light? Is it seen
against red or is it seen against blue?...This point
calls attention, however, to the question of objective
validity. In the classic parallax, there is no truth *per
se*, and the two scenarios in the diagram are entirely
relative to each other. But in our world, one view of
events may be the truer one, even if we don't quite
know which one that is. And through revelation, the
same could be said about the realm of the spirit.
Different people may be standing in different places,
but there may in fact be a *better* place to stand.

Nowhere is this split clearer than in the story
of Jesus. A man was born, and He grew up to pro-
claim His vision of the Kingdom of Heaven. Some
people listened to Him, decided to follow Him, and
eventually came to the awareness that He must be
the Lord in the flesh.[56] But others could only see in
Him a mortal threat to society, and they could think
of nothing better to do than nail Him to a tree. He
was thus murdered by a conspiracy of both Church
and State, Caiaphas and Pilate. The living God, or

---

[55] Alexander, "Sort by Controversial," *Slate Star Codex*.
[56] Matthew 16:16.

a criminal deserving of death: could there ever be a greater polarization of perspective than the one triggered by Jesus? But not all perspectives are equal here. We know that Jesus is what He said He was, and that the people who wanted to see Him dead were woefully deluded. The parallax is asymmetrical, then. People have different standpoints, but one of them happens to be correct, and to see Jesus as the Lord is better than to see Him in any other way.

The concept of parallax is almost endless in its riches. It emerges, for instance, in these prophetic words:

> God appears and God is light
> To those poor souls who dwell in night
> But does a human form display
> To those who dwell in realms of day.[57]

This world is the fallen one; but light is the primordial symbol of the power of Heaven, ever since early humans began to identify the Sun with a central deity of life-giving force. But there is a light behind light — a spiritual light — of which physical light is a metaphor. So on the one hand, in this world of ours that's really a type of Purgatory, divinity appears in the form of literal light; and on the other, when most folk envision the nature of the other world, they tend to think of pure light.

But we can go further. As our consciousness rises, the world changes in ratio, in the same sense that what looks like an anthill to a man would have the dimensions of a pyramid to an ant. Likewise, the cosmos appears to us as an abyss of incomprehensible

---

[57] Blake, "Auguries of Innocence," *Complete Writings.*

magnitude — but it might well look more like a home from the standpoint of a much larger imagination.[58] An unbreakable bond exists between the reality that is seen and the soul that does the seeing, such that as the soul transforms, so does the world. Perspective is everything. From our position on the ground, God looks like light — but this is strictly relative to the parallax angle from which we are viewing Him. If He is a few miles up in the sky, then we would only see Him from below. But as we elevate, the picture begins to change. What started as a vague abstraction morphs into something much more palpable and alive. The formless light begins to take on the contours of a recognizable shape; and by the time that we are high enough up to see God almost face to face, we realize that the light dwells in the form of a radiant Man. We may affirm that this position is the one that reveals the *most* about the Truth of the world.

DIAPHANOUS FLUX

We may hypothetically consider the world as an immanent geometric plane.[59] Every single person is then a nexus of energy with their own unique soular configuration, and that nexus is to be found at a specific locus within the plane. If this is how the world is, then there is no room at all to talk about universal, capitalized Truth. Rather, every person vibrates at their own frequency, and that energy bounces off others; and that's all there is to be said. Some interactions are called "love," some are called "enmity," some "indifference," and so on; and each flux

---

[58] Frye, *Fearful Symmetry*.
[59] Deleuze, *Pure Immanence*.

is just as valid as every other, since nothing dwells outside the field of energies itself. From within his own locus on the plane, a man might *say* that he has access to a reality that goes beyond the plane — but such an invocation would amount to a matter of mere *rhetoric*. To claim to know the Truth would be more or less the same as just declaring: "I am very, very serious about this part." It might be effective rhetoric, and it might win over some people while turning off others; but we would have no way to evaluate the point as such. Claiming to know the Truth is one energy, claiming to not know it is another, and all energies are equal.

We could call this picture the *horizontal* view of the world. My own mind is one system of signs among billions of such systems, and nothing I say could ever go beyond that system (since that would require leaving the horizontal plane altogether). If this is the lay of the land, then it would still be my prerogative — as a poet and a man — to try and create crystals of beauty that can persuade and attract others to my way of seeing things. If the horizontal plane is all there is, then we would be at liberty to make the most of it; and even if it is true that everything is arbitrary and relative, we would still be entitled to prefer our own frequency to any contenders.

But we must still consider the possibility that there is indeed such a thing as Truth, and that when we say Truth, we are not just referring to a particular node within our own semiotic systems. Many people today would deny this proposition, for our culture has long since decided that all metaphysics is unreal. But the sages across the ages have always affirmed the reality of the other realm, and the total rejection of this perennial vision is an anomaly that is quite unique to our late-modern times.[60] We are also obliged to observe that, from the standpoint of a circle, it would be difficult to understand a sphere. The circle would first have to enter into the sphere's mode of being, as it were; and in the meanwhile, the circle will probably call the sphere crazy, but the sphere must go on being itself.[61]

The horizontal world is home to the myriad glimmering phenomena we encounter every day and night of our lives. It is also home to the huge kaleidoscope of minds and perspectives and experiences that together make up the unfathomable complexity of our human race. What could I know of the life of someone who grew up on the other side of the ocean, or in a different carnal tent, or in times long since past or still yet to come? There is so much to appreciate in this banquet of differences — and the great merit of the horizontal view is that it is able to respect this panorama, let every taste be its own taste. Such an ethos is surely a vast improvement over the sort of dogmatism that insists that its own narrow and myopic slice of life is the only one that matters (for example, the sort of "religion" that has been too often used as a crude excuse for imperial conquest). But there are clearly also things we *can* know of each other, via the universality of the human condition. Radical differences may dwell at the surface; but farther down, people can always come to understand each other, assuming the presence of

---

[60] Huxley, *The Perennial Philosophy.*
[61] Abbott, *Flatland.*

intelligence and goodwill — since when all is said and done, our species is one in Adam Kadmon.[62]

We also have a problem down here, which is that the flat world can't sustain itself. The spiritual world is the source of energy for the physical world, the font of the waters of which this dimension is the delta. The horizontal perspective confines reality to the plane of immanence; as such, it rejects the reality of depth that is required if the spiritual realm is to ever appear to us, producing instead a *closed* world of limited energy. An increasing entropy and dis-integration will be the natural result of cutting off our own roots in spirit, since it is only through that channel that energy is replenished. Without a con-nection to spirit, we will burn up the fuel we have; then we will be running on fumes; and eventually we won't be running at all. Sooner or later, no mat-ter how good of a time we may be having, life will show us that the horizontal plane can't bear its own meaning. We will fail and suffer, people we love will leave us or die, and we will realize that we ourselves are going to perish. We will wonder, Buddha-like, what this life is for; and if we are unable to find a satisfactory answer, then only nihilism and despair will be left for us.

We must thus become enamored of vertical motion.[63] Life is a diaphanous flux, and the phys-ical world is a veil letting in the Light from Above. The immanent plane is not thus cancelled, but it gains depth, like a circle becoming a sphere. We may remember here the classic formula of seeing Jesus

---

[62] Fortune, *The Mystical Qabalah*.
[63] Vodalazhkin, *Laurus*.

in every person: the surfaces of our selves float on the horizontal plane, but the eternal image of God dwells within each of us, at the bottom of all depth. We may also think in terms of *sacramental perception.* Most pChurch folk would say that during the rite of the Communion, the bread and the wine turn into the flesh and blood of the living God — and they are absolutely right, of course; for when the intensity of imagination is raised to an incandescent pitch, the veil that separates this world from the other becomes more translucent than ever, and this world reveals itself as what it has been all along: a grand meta-phor for the realm of the soul.[64] From the mChurch standpoint, we might only add that such an experience could potentially happen anywhere, for what matters is the awakening of the living imagination. The Light from Above is able to burst forth into this world, preserving the variegated flux while at the same time ensconcing it all within new meaning and resonance. Everything comes alive again.

THE CULT OF THE GHOST

Since every cult needs a swashbuckling credo, let ours adopt this one: "Do not underestimate your own courage. You are part of an elite. Not of power, position, and wealth, but an elite of the sensitive, the considerate, and the tenacious. Its members are to be discovered in all castes, and throughout all ages; and among them there is a shared understanding. They represent a tradition of struggle against cruelty and unrelenting chaos. Thousands of them perish in

---

[64] Emerson, "Nature," *Essays & Lectures.*

obscurity, a few gain notoriety. They are sensitive for others as well as themselves, their consideration is without frills, their tenacity is not braggartly but has the power to truly endure, and above all they can accept the irony of their own fate."[65] What makes for a member of the cult of the Ghost, a person who's akin to a veteran of the soul? We may simply suppose that a man who dedicates his life to becoming a chef will probably turn out to be pretty excellent at creating a meal; and in the same way, a man who spends decades pursuing the living God might well end up learning a thing or two about Him in the process. It is just the sort of thing that sometimes happens when talent and sweat decide to merge.

In this day and age, any notion of superiority is only understood as offensive, a taboo, a thing that decent folk are not supposed to talk about. People are afraid to deal in absolutes, establish a scale of values. But such relativism is nothing but a ticking time bomb of its own contradictions, destined to implode — with any luck, sooner rather than later. When shall we internalize the point that the statement "There is no absolute Truth" is itself an absolute? Likewise, the idea that we are now beyond grand narratives is itself a form of narrative: "before" we believed in narratives, but *now* we are too good for them. And so on.[66] It is all too obvious that we humans are storytelling and meaning-making creatures, and that we have no way to step outside all such constructs. The refusal to make a decision is already one decision in particular, an avenue pursued at the expense of

[65] Bantock, *The Morning Star.*
[66] Jameson, *Postmodernism.*

the alternatives. So, if we are blessed or condemned to invent legends, then why not embrace the most beautiful and glorious ones that we can imagine? Why not let our souls take flight and think in terms of our deepest intuitions, rather than some blind and anemic concept of necessity or "reason"?

A vital poetic vision could well serve as a bridge into the future, beyond the collapse of our late modern world. In any event, life sure teaches us that the last part of that credo — the one about accepting the irony of our own fate — is crucial. In the world that we are obliged to live in, spiritual values do not track with their material counterparts. Much the opposite, in fact: it remains true that it is easier for a manatee to swim into a can of beer than for a rich man to buy a pass into the Kingdom of Heaven.[67] And the other way around: mastery of spirit by no means promises worldly success; if such success was what a man wanted, then he would just be playing the wrong game altogether.

We could look, for example, at the sort of "art" that goes big and sells these days. The Hollywood jackals have resorted to churning out abominations in one franchise after another, afraid of new ideas and the risk of lacking a built-in audience. They have also taken to raiding our childhoods, producing discordant remakes of classic films, which no one in his right mind would have thought to request.[68] On the literary front, people seem to have lost all sight of the grand tradition of art — either out of simple illiterate ignorance, or as the toxic fruit of an

[67] Matthew 19:24.
[68] Burton, *Dumbo*.

ideology that dismisses the greatest creative works of all time as nothing more than the fantasies of a certain privileged social class. Everything is degraded to a matter of personal "taste," no matter how crude or tasteless the tongue in question is. Art is reduced to mere ornament — a nice decoration to have around, we suppose, but for the most part produced by lazy dilettantes who couldn't find anything better to do with their lives: maybe they should have been bankers instead. The poetic vocation is dismissed as adolescent fantasy at best, psychotic delusion at worst; and no one really knows what our imaginations are for... As I speak of this state of affairs, do we not feel the inevitable resentment creeping in? To a man who is committed to the works of the living soul, the society and culture of our era can only provoke a visceral sense of outrage.

That's how it begins, anyway. But then the soular man looks around and realizes that outrage is the name of the most popular game in town; that just about everyone has flipped his lid over something or another; that *outrage is one helluva drug*, making people feel like little gods in the midst of their ecstatic indignation. It then becomes clear to him that all this anger doesn't solve a single thing, and that the Annunaki are thrilled to see the advent and perpetuation of such strife — after all, that's more blood and vital force for them. The understanding dawns that when the black rose of resentment blooms in his own heart, he loses his own connection with the holy: which is to say, he no longer even has a claim to make, since what prerogative he had was rooted in that conduit alone.

Such a man begins to realize that the mantle of the prophet has no power to save him; that it could lead to a hubris that is the direct precursor of an all-consuming resentment; that it could well make him less like the Lord and more like the Devil instead. And at that frontier, he may start to think things such as:

> But I am just an arm hanging in the sun
> That's as spiritual as I know how to be
> Said that's as spiritual as I know how to be[69]

Or maybe:

> And the things that I know
> Let them drift like the snow
> Let me dwell in the light that's above[70]

After climbing Jacob's Ladder a good ways up and then back down again, a soular man may want little more than to find a place to rest.[71] He may begin to grasp that it is best to let go of the prideful insistence on his own prerogative, and to instead accept the cosmic irony of everything that dwells upon this earth. But he might go on all the same to make like a nightingale and sing in the shipwreck: for that is just in his strange nature, built into the mysteries of the heart. &.

---

[69] Moonface, "Daughter of a Dove," *City Wrecker*.
[70] Cohen, *The Flame*.
[71] Genesis: 28-12.

II ❧ SOUL

THE AMOEBA PROTOCOL

Skepticism is rampant in these latter days: the heathens scoff at everything, and they think that makes them cool and brave. Is it not obvious that what such people lack most of all is the courage to believe in the unseen; the guts to make an existential wager and commit to the implications? They wait for evidence that will never come, for they simply won't relent from using the wrong *method*. They will never get anywhere unless they learn to turn away from the pretensions of modern science and rely on a more ancient road instead: the path of the poet. It is a matter not of reason, but of imagination. We must remember that when Jesus walked around upon this fallen land, most folk failed to recognize Him for who He was — and some failed so badly that they craved His death. Seeing the Truth for what He is has thus never been an easy or straightforward matter.[1] And that is because Truth is perceived not by the physical eyes, but rather only via the vision held within the heart.[2]

All kinds of false idols clamor for the loyalty of our imaginations, and a rightful skepticism should

---

[1] Kierkegaard, *Philosophical Fragments*.
[2] Saint-Exupéry, *The Little Prince*.

be directed at such ruses. But this is no reason to abandon the true cause as well. As one writer puts the matter: "But a child who relinquishes the illusions of Santa Claus, the Easter Bunny, and the Tooth Fairy, that child may come away with the most important skill set. That child may recognize the strength of his own imagination and faith. He will embrace the ability to create his own reality. That child becomes his own authority. He determines the nature of his world. His vision. And by doing so, by the power of his example, he determines the reality of the other two types: those who can't imagine, and those who can't trust."[3] The fact that the imagination can latch onto false content doesn't suggest that its power as such is any less real or wondrous. A lot of growing up just depends on aiming well: a man must learn how to use his imagination in much the same way that he learned to guide his arms and legs when he was just a child.

People in this late modern world seem very much like they are just trying to make the best of a bad time. They are incapable of the courage of faith, but they avoid this awareness by turning the script upside down and telling themselves that they're the ones who *really* know the score. They play a game of wearing paranoia as a badge of merit as they go about the world with the assumption that everything is lying to them. Love can't be love, for it must only be an illusion produced by chemical reactions; God can't be God, for there can only be a random entropy devoid of all meaning. And so on, to the point of nausea.

---

[3] Palahniuk, *Rant.*

This obsessive suspicion devours all the beauty and light that shines upon the earth — and then the fools who thought this was a good idea glory in their own nihilism.[4] Let us understand them for what they truly are: aspiring regicides against the living imagination; deniers of its primordial prerogative; abdicators of their own birthright as bearers of the image of God. We won't get very far until we commit to not listening to a word that emerges from the lips of such naysaying cowards.

The true imagination is the entire field of perception: everything we see drifts to and fro within that enchanted arena. It is a sort of aura or membrane, extended out from all the senses. It is also the fundamental organ of perception. No person really sees "with" his eyes or hears with his ears or feels with his skin. Rather, we sense *through* these things, as all the various windows of input converge in the unity and gestalt of an experience — and that agent of synthesis is none other than the living imagination.[5] We all know this to be true, if only we would dare to trust the way we actually experience this human existence. But some among us are unable to trust, and we thus think that life itself must be lying to us. Some among us are also unable to imagine, which is to say that they lack the sense for the inner depth of things. This sort of soular impoverishment can be seen everywhere in the ideologies that run our world today. We must reverse the perspective, give the holy imagination its proper due; for that is the only way to once again begin to live.

---

[4] Ricoeur, *Freud and Philosophy.*
[5] Blake, "Auguries of Innocence," *Complete Writings.*

The awakened imagination is like an amoeba: it wraps around all that exists, coloring everything with its own meaning and image.[6] In principle, there is *nothing* that stands outside this praxis of enchantment, just as no part of a man's life is outside of his own experience. The meaning in the world isn't given to the soul as such; rather, meaning is *built* via the power of imagination that engages with the scenario at hand. The more intense the imagination, the more alive the world is — the less intense, the more dead. We have no relevant way to judge the real and unreal except on the soular scale of life versus death.

A note of caution, however: done the wrong way, the amoeba protocol could perhaps go pretty schizo-phrenic, rather quickly. It is not a matter of "just" imagining whatever we want in order to make us feel better about an empty existence; it is also not about an emotional compensation by way of escape into a fantasy land. It is, instead, about taking the raw material of perception and raising it all to its highest level of radiance. We would probably need a *key* for this kind of gambit to actually work — and part of the good news is that we now have one. The Gospel is the pick for the skeleton lock, the pinnacle of all myth, where myth is not a lie but a sort of consolidated poetry, a storehouse of species wisdom illuminating the soular realm. But I'm afraid that this point can't be demonstrated to the imaginative heathens: the time for spectral argument is very far behind us. Poetic faith must follow its own prerog-ative, go its own way.[7]

---

[6] Frye, *Fearful Symmetry*.

[7] Blake, "Jerusalem," *Complete Writings*.

RAILROAD LANTERNS

The key Gnostic insight is that this world is a place from which to escape, just as the signature Christian idea is that people must be saved.[8] Many today may reject such propositions altogether — but to anyone who cares to look more deeply into things, it must become obvious that this world is a very broken realm, and that our lives themselves present us with a deep conundrum. This revelation of the dark is the genesis of any authentic search for the stronger light. Before we look for salvation, we must first of all realize that we stand in need of it; just as a jailbreak will never be possible so long as we imagine ourselves to already be free.

There may be an instinctual element to whether a man is inclined to see the world in this manner. Many people seem rather comfortable in their animal skins, needing no further explanation of life than what meets the mortal eye. Some in every generation, however, always seem to pass beyond such passive acquiescence and insist on seeing into the other realm. Maybe such men and women just have some dysfunction with their temporal lobes — the part of the brain associated with language, epilepsy, psychosis — and angels and demons struggle with each other for control of that turf. [9] Or maybe they receive a call from Above, like the prophets of yore: this is a well-attested phenomenon, in any event, and the fact that our world would like to ignore it is neither here nor there. We may suppose it is akin to a felt experience of heat (hellfire or holy fire — it

---

[8] John 3:17; Mead, *Pistis Sophia*.
[9] Garff, *Søren Kierkegaard: A Biography*.

is still hot), and it is probably the sort of thing that turns a man into either an inspired believer or else a lost cause.[10]

From our standpoint, we do not speak of "faith" in the ordinary sense of belief in the unseen. Rather, we speak of *vision*: the direct apprehension of what is more real than what the world calls real. No question of faith emerges here — at least, no more faith than what is required to believe that our loved ones are not hallucinations, or that we are in fact humans and not mere brains in vats. It is not about accepting abstract propositions, but rather a simple matter of trusting direct experience. We must also remain aware, however, of the fact that our merely mortal senses may deceive us; that they often conceal soular truth under a shell game of mirages. We must thus trust experience but also have discernment, become a fusion of dove and serpent.[11]

This point is perhaps the clearest of all in the Gospel. Jesus was not a man of exceptional looks, and nothing about his features would have elicited any particular comments from the people in his day and age.[12] Men and women and children were drawn to Him not because He looked like an actor or rock star, but only because of the demonstration of His life-giving deeds and words. This scenario is terrifying, if we think about it: the Lord Himself appears in this world in a form that had the inevitable design of concealing His true nature. Pagan gods were meant to look as powerful as they were; no gap existed

---

[10] Bon Iver, "Carved in Fire," 22, *A Million*.

[11] Matthew 10:16.

[12] Isaiah 52:3.

between their essence and their image. In contrast,
the God of the Gospel pushes the tension between
essence and image to its breaking point, revealing
just how little our physical eyes are worth when they
are divorced from soular vision.

Peering beneath the surface, we may learn things
that we may come to wish we hadn't. It becomes
obvious, for example, that the people who are most
dramatic and sentimental are most often the ones
who have no capacity at all for real feeling; that
they think of emotions as just so many levers for
manipulation.[13] We come to realize that with a dis-
concertingly large number of people, those are fangs
behind their smiles, and that most of what they do
is intended not to catalyze communion, but only to
give them an edge in the contest of self-interest.
Where was that person's hand a few hours before I
shook it — for that matter, where was mine? We must
love folk with lucidity and remember that we are not
exempted from the general law of sin, even as it is
probably also true that those who think about their
failures are spared from the bottom of the barrel by
that very awareness: for the worst sort of evil tends
not to worry about itself.

Things are nothing at all like what they seem down
here. We must learn to see with the eyes of the
heart and to look, as if by the lights of lanterns in
a tunnel, for the traces of truth that continue to run
through the infinite overwhelming falsehoods, the
latter being rotten fruits of archons who have made
it their mission to prevent us from ever waking up.
There is not even any need for totalitarian control

---

[13] Kundera, *The Unbearable Lightness of Being.*

anymore, seeing as most people are more than content with entertaining themselves unto oblivion, given the opportunity to merely be left alone while doing so.[14] It soon becomes evident that demonic influences are at work in this world, and that the Devil is engaged in a perpetual project of entrapment.[15] We begin to understand that we all start off as slaves to this world, and that a lot of life has to do with realizing this fact and then trying to do something about it. The Gospel may then appear to us as a sort of Underground Railroad, a clandestine apparatus that was built with the intention of smuggling slaves out of the dark and into freedom.

GENETICS AND ANGEL'S BLOOD

An intriguing query to put forth on the Internet is: "Whence emerged the Y chromosome of Jesus?" It is a worthy question on the merits. We accept that Jesus was conceived by the Holy Ghost; but the Ghost is a being of spirit, and He thus presumably is not in possession of chromosomes. If Jesus was fully human, though, He must have had a full human complement of our DNA. He received His X chromosome from His mother Mary, of course; but then, if He had no human father, how did He get the Y that made Him a man? What would a genetic test of Jesus have shown? We should probably rule out asexual processes that are most often reserved for reptiles and invertebrates — rather unbecoming for the highest form of life there ever existed. The situation thus remains a mysterious one.

---

[14] Postman, *Amusing Ourselves to Death*; Wallace, *Infinite Jest*.
[15] Lewis, *The Screwtape Letters*.

An anecdote: I have often had a bone-deep intuition that my alleged biological dad could not have
been my father. There is an obvious alternative, which
is that I could have been a bastard. But if I were
a bastard, then my mother must have done things
that she morally could not have done. So perhaps I
was a sort of virgin birth, and my real father was
an angel? — not among the seraphim or anything,
but just some workaday, run-of-the-mill angel...
It may seem that I speak in jest, but this type of
whimsical thought process can help us broach the
subject of what exactly happened at the moment of
the Incarnation. In order to go further, we will need
to establish the superiority of poetry over science.
Science is about the investigation of the realm of
matter; and at that level, if Jesus was a man (and
He was), then He must have had a genetic code in
congruence with a male of the species. But that is not
germane to the claim at hand, and the presence of a
Y chromosome in Jesus should not be taken to imply
that it came from a human father. We are talking
here about an *abrogation* of the "facts" by a greater
power — and that power is the poetic imagination.

From the standpoint of poetry, the material world
is a metaphor, and the truths of the soul rank higher
than the facts of the flesh. But the facts of the body
could sometimes conceal a deeper reality rather than
directly letting the latter shine forth; and at that
point, it might become needful to rely on paradox
and let poetry have its prerogative. We are speaking
of an appeal to an altogether different order of reality: a dimension that plays by its own rules, having
nothing at all to do with naive science. The blood's

revolt is sometimes worth more than all the anemic "facts" in the world.[16]

This line of thought leads us to a unique sympathy for people who identify as transgender — those who believe that they were born in a wrongly sexed body. At the level of science, a person was born in a man's body; but at the level of poetry, his imagination insists that he must really be a woman. There is some obvious resonance between this notion and my whimsical musing on angelic descent. But the transgender theory also suffers from a crucial error: namely, the fact that it doesn't appeal to another dimension of reality, but rather insists that imagination can negate this carnal realm as such. It declares that if a man identifies as a woman and gets the cosmetic alterations required to pass for one, then he must for all intent and purpose be well and truly a woman. One problem here is that to "pass" as something one isn't would be an act of deception. We may also observe the outright misogyny of such a view: for it suggests that there is nothing more essential to being a woman than just looking like one at the level of skin.

The pursuit of chemical alteration and even surgery would then be akin to a man declaring that he has angel's blood — and that he must therefore glue plastic wings upon his back in order to belabor the point and persuade others to validate his self-conception. That's not it. That's not it at all. That would be what one theologian calls *angelism* — the disorder of dissociating from the parameters of physical

---

[16] Dostoevsky, *Notes from Underground.*

existence.[17] Likewise, we could understand not quite wanting to live in *any* body at all, forget its sex. Of course, turning to suicide to "fix" that problem would be unacceptable counsel. Our sympathy thus cannot translate into endorsement; for to endorse a delusion is an act of cruelty, and any compassion worthy of the name consists of talking an unwell person off his own cliff, not encouraging him to take the plunge. My line of thought, then, is not to be confused with this sort of thing. It is a different kind of proposition, having to do with the metaphysical genesis of our species and the rivalry among different orders of knowledge.

From a broader vista, all of us humans resemble fallen angels — in our spiritual forms, we may well have wings, their size and power and splendor changing in relation to our level of soular development.[18] Some among us, however, may have an inherent connection with the angels that goes beyond this general claim. The Father in Heaven is the father of us all, but Jesus is also the Son of God in a unique and personal sense. In an infinitely lesser manner, a pneumatic — natural breather of spirit — may sense a tie with the angels so strong that his soul might well begin to insist that it is akin to a *filial* bond. Creative men and women have been known to have such thoughts, and we shouldn't feel ashamed to toss in our lots with them.[19] A poetic truth dwells in this conception, and we could do worse than to peer beyond its veneer of madness.

---

[17] Maritain, *Dream of Descartes*.
[18] Unknown Friend, *Meditations on the Tarot*.
[19] Dylan, *Chronicles*; Fitzgerald, *The Great Gatsby*.

FACES EVERYWHERE

Some folk imagine that the people of the distant past must have had access to psychedelics, and that this is how they were able to enter into the wild visions that led to the emergence of the religions and spiritual traditions of the world. I see their point: after all, it is impossible to read the Book of Revelation without at least considering the notion that the man was on a rather intense trip. The same could be said for the prophets — Ezekiel in particular comes to mind, what with his vision of four-faced creatures and the blazing wheels with many eyes.[20]

This hypothesis may contain a modicum of truth; but on the balance, I find it needless as an explanatory model. Rather, what is probably the case is that way back when, people just had more direct access to alternate modes of consciousness, since technocratic reason had not yet emerged and made its claim to be the only thing that's real. Maybe those people were able to tap into something like the dream state at will; maybe that frequency was in fact their *norm*. Three-dimensional spacetime had not quite settled yet, and people would have lived in a wavier nexus — sort of like what sometimes happens when we get into our cups, or the effect produced by certain techniques of animation.[21] Small wonder, then, that people had visions. They would have lived in a mythical, enchanted dimension of mind where much of the world was still alive with meaning, and where few would have even thought to question the reality of the gods.

---

[20] Ezekiel 1:4-21.
[21] Linklater, *Waking Life*.

There is an animism that we could identify as the original religion of humankind, centered on the archetypes of the sky god and the earth goddess.[22] Such a tradition evolved over time into a panentheism where the singular God, font of all being, both suffuses this world and surpasses its limits; and to some extent, this consolidation is the claim to fame of the biblical tradition of the prophets, which of course reaches its apotheosis in the Gospel. Animism is the belief that the whole world is alive with spirits; and while we do not reject this premise, we must also insist that the one true Lord is the Creator of all, that He lives within the depths of the heart, and that He is the focus of our devotion — whatever other spirits surely populate this realm.

Of course, this whole line of thought will be lost on many of the denizens of our world. Folk today are inclined to believe that the people of the past were just projecting their own internal lives onto the world, thereby distorting its nature in the process. On this account, seeing the world for what it is would require a man to withdraw such imaginings and look at things in a state of *disenchantment* — a powerful watchword for the whole modern ethos.[23] But such a demand is an offense against the prerogative of the imagination electric, and we must resist its imperative. We will always affirm that the world grows *more* and not less real when we see it in an enchanted manner. The imagination seeks incarnation into the world; it needs to bond with the things in that world; and it wants to re-create external reality in its own poetic

---

[22] Paglia, *Sexual Personae*.
[23] Taylor, *A Secular Age*.

image. The line that began with animism and found its way to the prophets must live on, for everything depends on this persistence.

What do we see when we look up at the sky? The men and women who first invented the constellations must have witnessed a splendor that most of us could scarcely imagine (even if we could make the urban light pollution go away, which is a task in itself). They might have seen actual figures in motion, radiating energy and lending credence to all the mythical stories of yore. Perhaps they did not really have to "try" to see such things, since that cognitive mode was already natural to them.[24] They may have understood time as a wheel and space as a dreamscape. Dwelling in such an imaginal world, constellations could well have just presented themselves on their own.

"How do you know but every bird that cuts the airy way is an immense world of delight, closed by your senses five?"[25] And how do we know but that every cloud is the shadow of an angel, sending some magic our way if only we would agree to participate? Our extremist adherence to secular reason has robbed us of so much of our true species birthright and heritage.[26] We could take it all back any time we wanted — although we might well have to ignite a brushfire in our minds, in order to clear away all the accumulated detritus. We must dig deeper if we are to access the wisdom of days long gone by. At that point, we might find ourselves in the shoes of one brave man who experienced a transformation of the

---

[24] Gebser, *The Ever-Present Origin.*
[25] Blake, *The Marriage of Heaven and Hell.*
[26] Jacobs, "After Technopoly," *The New Atlantis.*

very sky: "Don't I know that it is infinite space and not a round vault? But no matter how I squint and strain my sight, I cannot help seeing it as round and limited, and despite my knowledge of infinite space, I am undoubtedly right when I see a firm blue vault, more right than when I strain to see beyond it."[27] That's exactly how it is; anyone could access it (as soon as we tell the hyenas in our heads to be quiet) and begin to see with the eyes of the heart instead. This is the decision of imagination over reason, poetry over science. Do we dare to see men in the clouds and women in the trees? Do we dare to let the great dance light up all of reality? There are faces everywhere, if only we learned again how to notice them.

At the end of this train of thought, we may well come to understand that there is no external world per se; that the world is always relative to a particular perceiver; and that if all such perceivers were eliminated, then that would be the end of the world as well. The world shows itself in a particular way to us humans; and since we are the bearers of the image of God, the whole cosmos knows itself through us — and through the most visionary of us the best. If no humans were left, then that would trigger a full-scale *gestalt collapse*, and the world itself would revert to a deader and less radiant state. We cannot fathom such a scenario, since we can't possibly know how this world would look if we weren't here to enchant it with our species imagination. The Lord must have been crazy to have gifted us fallen creatures with such a vast responsibility and mandate — and yes, that sort of madness is very much His way.

---

[27] Tolstoy, *Anna Karenina*.

HOLDING UNION STATION

It is incredible to think about how so much of everything we see around us in our lives has been built by humans. The roads, the lights, the buildings, the tech — none of it was there before the fact. All of it was made as a result of the creative power of the human soul, from conception to incarnation. To look around us with adequate sensitivity is to always already witness an unfolding magic spell. Not all of it is beautiful, of course; but even the creation of ugly things is only a perversion testifying to a deeper reality, just as the Devil can't help but speak to the glory of the Lord. And the human mind is no less miraculous, what with its capability to absorb endless material from the world and to re-constitute all of that input into its own image of truth.

What is the individual imagination? It resembles a grand train station — rather like the ones that were so important in the Romantic era — with every train of thought (ahem) flowing into the center and then departing, all in accordance with the mercurial schedules of life here in this dimension. The mind could well be dubbed Union Station, given the huge activities of synthesis that go on within it at all times to hold the soul together. The stuff of the world flows in, takes care of its business, and then flows out again; all the while, the mind is receiving incoming trains and sending out its own trains in the form of real-time words, gestures, expressions.

The literal train system is a massive and elegant infrastructure, just like the highways; and there is almost something Gothic in the way that it often developed out of a quasi-organic creative impetus to meet the needs of the people. So much splendor dwells in what our collective species imagination has wrought. But natural disasters — or some greater cataclysm — could knock it all offline at any given moment, reduce all our pretty constructions to rubble. The order of collective species imagination, also known as *civilization,* lives in perpetual struggle against the pulls of darkness and chaos that threaten to reduce creation to the entropic abyss from which it first emerged.[28] And the same danger threatens the single human imagination as well. These days, the world refers to such a problem as mental illness; but we should really be partial to the more old-school notion of *sin.* That undertow is part of the brokenness built into the human condition, and it stands in need not of "treatment" but redemption.

Sin, indeed, results in the death of the imagination, since sin is like an earthquake that strikes the station of the mind — with the Richter count rising depending on the severity of the act. Sin clouds the entire field of perception, makes it impossible for a man to engage in honest and transparent relations with the people in his life, the world around him, and the Power that established him.[29] The earthquake sends the tracks into disrepair — if it is *really* bad, then the entire station could get knocked off the grid. A man becomes incapable either of receiving input from the world or sending messages out; he becomes locked within the dungeons of his own private head.

We needn't look far for case studies. Pornography

---

[28] Moonface, "Return to the Violence of the Ocean Floor," *Organ Music Not Vibraphone Like I'd Hoped.*
[29] Kierkegaard, *The Sickness unto Death.*

is a good example of the problem: after seeing such images, it is almost impossible for the viewer to look at actual women with an honest gaze until the aftershock of sensation wears off. The bestial pleasure functions to ruin the clarity of vision, as a man grows lost in phantasms and cut off from his true and relational self. Excessive drug use can also produce a chemical stupor, a tremor that disables a man's system and life force for a couple of days or more. These are only examples. In reality, the threats are everywhere, and the soular call requires vigilance. More sensitive people may suffer more deeply from sin: for they actually feel the earthquakes and their consequences; whereas a lot of folk appear to have the ambiguous fortune of being able to proceed with their lives and not notice very much. It is a sign of maturity when the theoretical wages of sin become a palpable reality, and when sin makes us feel that we are passing into literal death.[30]

The total collapse of the mind's train system — a massive earthquake — is generally what's meant by the onset of psychosis. It is when the imagination is no longer able to function as the nexus of vast energies and instead becomes flat and dull, loses its bounce. Such a thing also tends to happen with an experience of trauma, which signifies a train coming in that is so strange and fast and foreign that the station of the mind is unable to accommodate it, with the result being a wreck, until and unless the owner of that station can figure out how to make space for the new state of affairs.

---

[30] Romans 6:23; Hesse, *My Belief.*

As a man comes to understand the mortal threat presented by such disturbances to Union Station, he may begin to search for a keystone, a foundation, that grants immunity against such a thing ever happening again. He may seek a way to ensure that the station is held. Such a man may be led by raw intuition to these blunt words: "In Him was life, and the life was the light of men. And the light shines in the darkness, and the darkness did not overcome it."[31] Ideas may be bulletproof, and maybe manuscripts don't burn, but the incarnate Light from Above is outright immortal.[32] We may thus speak of the *soular utility* of the Gospel: when a man needs to save his own life, he finds that the good news simply works, and all further considerations turn pale and fade into irrelevance. Such a man may also begin to understand that art may be rather impotent — for, after all, people write masterpieces and then still kill themselves.[33] It becomes evident that what is really needed is a theurgical *art of salvation* keyed to the conditions of human existence.[34]

THE ALAMO OF THE SOUL

The Battle of the Alamo was an important episode in a famous revolution.[35] A bunch of Texans were hunkered down in the Alamo — a mission fortress — to make a stand against the Mexicans. The Texans were destroyed down to almost the last man, suggesting

---

[31] John 1:4-5.
[32] McTeigue, *V for Vendetta*; Bulgakov, *The Master and Margarita*.
[33] Max, *Every Love Story is a Ghost Story*; Rank, *Art and Artist*.
[34] Berdyaev, *The Meaning of the Creative Act*.
[35] Fehrenbach, *Lone Star*.

a complete and utter defeat. But then something unexpected happened. The fall of the Alamo became a rallying point for all the rest of the Texans (and hence emerged the slogan to remember it). The paradoxical morale boost produced by this disastrous battle swept the Texans to victory in the overall war. An apparent defeat that mutates into an actual victory in the end: well, this pattern should be familiar to any Christian, since the Gospel is all about a loss on the Cross that turned out to be an ultimate win in the Cave. Would it be fair for us, then, to speak of the Alamo of the soul?

This world is so deceptive when it comes to such matters. We measure success in the crass terms of money and power; and by those standards it is almost always the worst of us who come out on top. It is a truism, for example, that no one who wants to be president should be allowed to run for the office; for no one but a megalomaniac or sociopath would desire to have such power over the lives of others. Likewise, the richest people are generally those who decided that money is more important to them than anything else. To have such lusts in proper working order is often a prerequisite for being successful in this world. And when it comes to that sort of project, having a soul is a positive liability; for such a thing introduces an additional dimension of concern which could well introduce barriers against the pursuit of naked self-interest and the will to power. The less of a soul a man has, then, the more cut out he is for "success" on the terms of the world. A man like that will never have to get distracted by the sayings of Jesus, such as: "Blessed are the meek, for they shall inherit the earth."[36] If we want the world to call us winners, then it would surely be better to not think about such matters.

The perspective shifts, however, when we understand that there is a war going on in this world; that the war is soular in nature; and that victory in that war is the highest priority of this life. Little common ground exists between the people who see this reality and those who do not; each would ultimately have to consider the other mad, for the first premises are just too different from each other. Such vision was the original basis of the distinction between the pagan and the Christian, and it is also why the Christian is not a natural man.[37] We must be born again from battle, re-created in the heat of soular struggle. This is surely at least one meaning of the baptism by fire — which, incidentally, has an uncanny resonance with the hopes and dreams of ancient alchemy.

Going through our lives, we also start to grasp that the world is indeed hostile to the project of building the soul. Sometimes it turns into a matter of outright murderous anger, as it does near the end of the gospels; but more often, it is a matter of just being ignored or laughed at, the small everyday humiliations, the continuous casual rejection of what matters most to us.[38] We may try to act like it is nothing; but, all the while, we know that this isn't right and this isn't just. On darker days, desperate words such as these may well resonate with us:

---

[36] Matthew 5:5.
[37] 1 Corinthians 2:14.
[38] Vaneigem, *The Revolution of Everyday Life.*

I must soon declare my war on their war
I must hold to my last piece of ground
I must protect the small space
I have made that has allowed me life[39]

An instinct arises to let us know for certain that the rules of this world are made of dust, and that its platitudes are worse than meaningless. We realize that there is nothing to do in this life but to find what is true in us and then defend it to the last breath, whatever the consequences. We come to understand that nothing matters more than holding the Alamo of the soul — and that, even if we are taken down, the greater design is already in motion.

The body and the spirit are supposed to be one, united in the living and incarnate soul. But if that is so, then why are the rules so radically divergent in the two realms, to the very point that death of the flesh could result in life of the spirit? Something is broken in this human condition; there must indeed have been an unfathomable Fall. We hunger for a justice where what is true in the realm of the spirit also becomes manifest in this material world. But reality often has different ideas. Down here, physical beauty in a person can be a mere veneer concealing a vast depravity of soul — just as beauty of the soul can be tied to a physical form that provokes repugnance in all passersby.[40] Something within us revolts and tells us that this cannot be the final state of affairs, that things must be different in the Kingdom; but, in the meanwhile, we are obliged to live in this dimension

---

[39] Bukowski, "A Challenge to the Dark," *Betting on the Muse*.
[40] Wilde, *The Picture of Dorian Gray*; Shelley, *Frankenstein*.

and navigate such tensions without imbibing the venom of resentment.

At a local show that I once saw in the city that's home to the Alamo, a random musician suggested that life is not a race but more of a rodeo: not a matter of going fast and winning, but rather all about *just hanging on*. From the standpoint of the soul, there isn't much of anywhere to go — and as the years pass, the world may well just seem more and more antagonistic, as the resistance turns out to be the same though our energies begin to wane. Maybe there is little to be done but to just hold the bastion until the game is over and know that this was a good way to live. The saints and the martyrs have done it before, after all, following in the footsteps of the man who did it forever. In spite of any letdowns, the high points of beauty and innocence and wonder surely exist; and those epiphanies should be quite enough by which to set our star charts. We should be willing to lose the battle and know that we've won the war.

DEMON DOJO

I can somewhat understand how people fail to believe in the gods — but it requires entirely another level of denseness to not believe in the demons. Who could look at our world and not know that demons are real? This world is broken; and despite our best efforts, we humans often seem unable to live up to our better angels, always falling instead under the influence of some irresistible undertow. Bad ideas possess people sometimes, and perhaps now more than ever.[41] Such a malady is the probable conse-

---

[41] Dostoevsky, *Demons*.

quence of people losing the ordinary anchors by which they were once able to gain some orientation within the world.[42] One of the most valid points raised by conservatism is that cultural traditions can be gauged by their survival value: if a tradition has existed for a very long time and enabled the people within it to thrive, then the face-value implication is that it is in basic congruence with reality, and that care should be taken before tearing it down.[43] Before we open ourselves to newness, we should take due diligence to ensure that the new in question is not possessed by demons that are more horrific than the ones found in the present we inhabit.

This point, however, is by no means intended as a defense of the status quo. It is only a criticism of novelty for its own sake, or an adolescent passion that has failed to take the full picture into account. This present work is an attempt to help break new ground. Indeed, the irruption of the new into this world is the very purpose of this dimension of reality, with the Incarnation serving as the fundamental archetype. The game is thus surely not about passively letting the old have its own way. Rather, the idea is that, in order for something new to truly matter and have traction, it must wrestle with its own tradition, like Jacob with the angel.[44] To build something new is to first of all have a thorough comprehension of what came before.

One way or the other, the new must come, for the darkness that dwells in this world cannot be

---

[42] Bauman, *Liquid Modernity*.
[43] Chesterton, *Collected Works, Volume III*; Kirk, "Ten Conservative Principles," The Russell Kirk Center.
[44] Genesis 32:28.

permitted to persist. Demons live here in the present within the historical Church, and hence the
imperative need for prophecy; we have to engage
in a continual insurrection of drawing spirit into
the world and challenging ossified structures that
have betrayed their original mission. Jesus shook up
the synagogues, and those who aspire to act in His
name should likewise strive to carry on the perennial
project of the prophets. We also do not need to stick
to the macro-level about these matters. In the life of
the individual soul, the demons are often the first to
show themselves to any man who's sensitive to such
things. This may begin to happen around the onset
of adolescence — the point at which spirit begins to
feel a strange attraction to the human personality.[45]
A man may find, for instance, that he must struggle
to overcome the hauntings imparted to him by his
own circumstances and upbringing, so that he may
grow in the direction of what the soular impetus
commands him to become.

Sooner or later, we are forced to understand that
to refuse the imminent fight with the demons is
inevitably to succumb to them. We can either struggle
against our demons or consent to being governed by
them, with no third option on the table. There is the
shadow play, and then there is the grace, and the
latter is always waiting for us; but until we deal with
the closets and traumas that populate our own souls,
the Light from Above will just have no way to enter.
A good soular instinct can usually detect a demon,
with the toxin serving as a tocsin and producing a

---

[45] Pullman, *His Dark Materials*.

wake-up call. But the demons are more present than a naif might imagine — and moreover, not all demons are personal. Most of them may actually be part of the *collective* unconscious; and if a man is in a weakened state of mind, they might take the opportunity to overwhelm him while his defenses are down. It is rightly said that true character reveals itself under stress, and that we don't know what people would do if they found themselves in such a scenario. Perhaps they could do anything, for just about anything is possible without soular integrity; and the ordinary human herd instinct is very strong indeed.

The demons make us suffer, and some people seem to think of the reality of such darkness in our realm as evidence in the infernal prosecutor's case against the Lord. But is it not obvious that suffering plays a crucial role in the evolution of a man, and that without such experience, a man might exist in the undead state of some sort of fratty Neanderthal forever? A famous quote is worth repeating here: "He who learns must suffer. And even in our sleep, pain that cannot forget falls drop by drop upon the heart; and in our own despair, against our will, comes wisdom to us by the awful grace of God."[46] We must become willing to enter the demon dojo and declare open combat with our own shadows.[47] What are the things that haunt us? What forces prevent us from rising to the highest heights of our own destinies? Over time, we may well realize that the fight makes us strong, and that to know and battle against our demons is to gain a self-knowledge that

---

[46] Aeschylus, *Oresteia*.
[47] Jung, *Aion*.

eventually grows unshakeable. This is how we come to understand ourselves, and it is also how we learn not to take out our own darkness on all unsuspecting innocents in the vicinity. It is difficult work, to be sure; but sooner or later, it begins to pay dividends as the fields of our energies morph in tandem with our own best intentions.

SPIRIT SICKNESS

To think about the poet is to reflect on the duality of sky and earth. The poet is a man of imagination, and he soars like an albatross across the skies of the soul. But the poet is also notorious for often being rather dysfunctional in his worldly life, sometimes to the point that he could well be slapped with multiple psychiatric diagnoses from the heathen scripture known as the DSM.[48] Ordinary existence is lived on the earth — and the poet, with his huge wings, may have trouble with walking.[49] It is *because* of his wings that he cannot walk; and conversely, many people are very comfortable down here exactly because they lack the requisite equipment for aviation. This is a grand cosmic irony.

Some powers may come with an inherent, self-destructive handicap; such a dynamic can be found all over the place. *Take one*: the martyrs all died because of their soular will to follow Jesus and His Gospel, which is to say that they had to give up their lives in order to have life. *Take two*: a fictional mutant has almost indestructible strength — but he hurts himself every time he uses his power, and he

---

48 Kundera, *Life Is Elsewhere*.
49 Baudelaire, "The Albatross," *The Flowers of Evil*.

has trouble forming any real connections with others.[50] *Take three*: Jacob wrestled with the Angel, and he came out of it lamed for life — but this is also when he was christened Israel, the head of an entire race of men.[51] *Take four*: one of the greatest poets of the ancient age was known to be blind: he could see because he couldn't see.[52] We could go on, but I suppose that the point has sufficiently come across.

A prophet may be described as more or less a poet gone universal: for whereas the poet may be content with speaking a subjective truth and leaving things be, the prophet draws out the implications for our entire species. What begins as a poetic venture could turn into prophecy over time. The poet, digging deep into his soul, may arrive at a juncture where he realizes that all souls are one and that in talking about his own soul, he is in fact also shining a light upon the universal Soul. But such a path can surely take its toll. Here is one sage's take on this dynamic: "A prophet is a sick man. A prophet is an invalid of the sort who has lost the healthy, sound, beneficent instinct of self-preservation, which is the essence of all middle-class virtues. There must not be many of these men; otherwise the world would go to pieces. He is a manic, a seer. In him a section of the world has developed a rare, noble, and vulnerable organ that others do not have — that in the case of all the rest, for their health and happiness, has remained vestigial."[53] Something about such a man, then, has a strange compensation

---

50 Mangold, *Logan*.
51 Genesis 32:28.
52 Homer, *The Odyssey*.
53 Hesse, *My Belief*.

built in. The talents of the prophet and his drawbacks can't be readily separated from each other; they come together, the gift and the curse. There is thus a rather good reason that most folk stay away from this path, and such timid judgment calls out for not scorn but a certain level of respect.

No criterion exists to determine whether a man is worthy of such a calling. In fact, the common notion of worthiness may not even apply in cases such as these. The Lord's judgment follows the pattern of choosing Noah the drunkard to save the human race and David the lecher to be the king of the chosen people — which is to say that He has a way of choosing some deeply flawed men to carry out His work.[54] On the terms of this world, though, the prophet may find himself to be a rather unworthy man. His inherent sensitivity could make him ill and unable to live in the ordinary sense of the word.[55] He may feel like a veteran trying to adjust to civilian life, not at all sure of what he's supposed to do with himself. And our world as it stands, for its part — utterly blind to the destinies of hearts — has no place whatsoever for prophecy; indeed, it can only insist that any such notion must be a symptom of burgeoning mental illness.

An inherent manic depression, a soular lunacy, is perhaps built into the prophet's venture, seeing as he does another world that is present but not yet incarnate. The proper channel for this desire would be a total transformation of this fallen earth — but of course, that would require the cooperation of

---

[54] Genesis 9:20; 2 Samuel 11:2.
[55] Houellebecq, *The Possibility of an Island.*

everyone else, which is often not forthcoming. The creative impulse may thus rebound into the prophet's volatile head, which then exacerbates the tensions already associated with having a unique antenna. Small wonder, then, that the prophets have tended to be unhappy men.[56] But this melancholia also tends to grant night vision: an owl-like ability to see in the dark and get to the heart of what life is about. We mustn't forget that the Crucifixion precedes the Resurrection — which is to say that whatever new life there is, it only dwells on the far side of a tunnel of immense suffering.

The prophet always understands that the Lord may save us, but that His first promise is to destroy what we think we are, insofar as our egos are opaque and false. Or rather, the deity's intention is to allow us to destroy ourselves, like magnificent pots smashed to pieces against the hard earth of sin. Then He appears with golden lacquer to build the pots up again anew, with the visible cracks only making them more beautiful.[57] Those pots are our own souls. The prophet knows this after passing through the spirit sickness for himself. In the end, this is the fate of all humans who insist on walking the soular path in the midst of a world gone to shit. If it were easy, would it be worth it?

ON BEAUTIFUL LOSERS

The prosperity gospel must be the worst heresy known to humankind. If *that* was all that people ever

---

[56] Jeremiah 15:10.
[57] Dreher, "The Gift of Kintsugi Christianity," *The American Conservative*; Bob-Waksberg, "Good Damage," *BoJack Horseman*.

heard about the Christian faith, then we couldn't blame them for being filled with revulsion at the prospect: for the folk who would use the name of Jesus to promote their own worldly agendas are among the worst our species has to offer. They are the ones who suggest that being rich is a sign of God's favor and an entry pass into the Kingdom — in direct contradiction with Jesus's most explicit sayings.[58] They seek to win power in this world and expand their principalities. And even the less awful members of that crowd fatally confuse Christendom with the Gospel: they want something called "Christian civilization" to prevail, regardless of whether it has anything to do with Jesus and with little thought for whether they are betraying Him in their headlong pursuit of success.

By the lights of the Gospel, this world functions on a demonic scale of values: it is power rather than truth that prevails down here. Truth is aerial, but power, like the world, is earthbound. The pursuit of truth thus need not translate into power at all. Much the opposite: truth could well take a man farther and farther up and away from the mandates of power, to the point that the world may sooner or later consider him dangerous or mad. Jesus was abandoned by His friends and condemned to death, as powerless as the infant in the manger He once was. He did win in the end, of course — but we must be very clear about what that entails. We say He won because He did what was needful, with unfailing fidelity, in order to secure the soular Truth: He sacrificed any and all

---

[58] Luke 18:25; Matthew 20:16.

power, along with His whole literal life, in order to make that happen. To the eyes of this world, however, Jesus was and must remain a failure; for what other sort of man would die on a cross like a common criminal? The logic is brutally simple.

There is another trap here as well, which has to do with the world's converse error of thinking that Jesus must be a winner because over the course of the centuries His mission spread across the entire earth; that Jesus was a success after all because some man named Constantine decided to adopt Christianity as the religion of his empire.[59] But we must know that this sort of "victory" is altogether irrelevant to the Gospel — and, indeed, that it could actually imperil souls; for it deludes people into believing that they are "Christian" merely because they were born into such a civilization.[60] It would be much better for heathens of the heart to at least know that they don't follow Jesus.

The Crucifixion was an event where all men turned against the scapegoated victim; but the victim — through an alchemy unknown before Him — flipped the script and revealed to the world the full horror of what it was.[61] After Calvary, we can no longer claim to not know; for the truth rose up from our collective unconscious and presented itself in dramatic form right before our eyes. The temptation to turn away from that awareness, however, is omnipresent; for on the terms of this world, Jesus could never

---

[59] MacCulloch, *Christianity: The First Three Thousand Years.*
[60] Kierkegaard, *Concluding Unscientific Postscript.*
[61] Girard, *I See Satan Fall like Lightning;* Moonface, *This One's for the Dancer & This One's for the Dancer's Bouquet.*

be anything more than the most beautiful of losers. To put principle before power means that, at some point, we must be willing to concede defeat on the grounds that we are not willing to pay the price to win — the price of the soul, that is. Amoral men will thus always have an advantage in this regard, since they have no inconvenient beliefs that limit their scope of possibilities for action. There are things that a decent man would just never do, but this is not true of the villain: he could, in theory, do *anything* in order to pursue his own self-interest. If a man has few scruples, then he will probably do well in this world; and if he has none, then he might become the president. But if he has them all, he may just end up on desolation row along with all the rest of the broken prophets.[62]

Many people are willing to kill for what they consider the truth: they will conquer by the sword if they must, and they will say that what they do is right and good. For us, this option is just not really on the table. We might die for the Truth if required, but we could never kill in its name — for, as Jesus said, we must put the literal sword away and only wield the sword of the spirit.[63] Therefore, if a juncture emerges between either accepting a worldly loss or using heinous means in order to win, we should choose against the latter. Because of that, the bad guy could well win in the short run, since he is not inhibited by such qualms. The Gospel thus forces a decision upon us: when the sky is at odds with the earth, which way will we cut? It would be

[62] Dylan, "Desolation Row," *Highway 61 Revisited*.
[63] Matthew 26:52 & 10:34.

wonderful for truth to get translated into power in a direct manner; but, alas, that isn't the aerial world that we live in quite yet.

We must decide which is more real to us — the Kingdom or this dimension. And we are called to make the requisite sacrifices in the event that power proves to be incompatible with fidelity to the Truth. In the long run, the aerial game is always worth it, and nothing but dust awaits those who are enamored with power; for power is always vain and mortal. It is also true that the soul is the foundation, and that a civilization that succumbs to the nihilism of power has already signed its own death warrant.[64] Such knowledge doesn't make the soular life much easier in the meanwhile. A prime source of comfort, however, is remembering Jesus's declaration that this realm hated Him long before it ever caught sight of us.[65] And walking this path, we may one day learn that "winning" is highly overrated, and that the victory of the living soul is the only one that matters. The result of this enchantment should be a heart filled with joy and not sorrow: a joy having little to do with either the blessings or the curses of this deluded world.

THE LOGIC BOMB

A generic dictionary's definition of a logic bomb is: "A set of secret instructions incorporated into a program so that if a particular condition is satisfied, they will be carried out, usually with harmful effects."[66] Well, then: we can understand the Gospel

---

[64] Barzun, *From Dawn to Decadence*.
[65] John 15:18.
[66] Words API.

as a logic bomb built into the code of the human soul — from the Devil's perspective, that outcome surely is catastrophic. A man may get to a point in his mind where it seems like no light remains and all soular work has been in vain.[67] Jesus Himself must have seen that precipice, first while sweating blood in Gethsemane and then when spilling it at Calvary, wondering why He had been forsaken.[68] Was it all worth anything at all? But that nadir is also the prime lever for a total reversal. At the very moment that the Devil thinks he has won, he is compelled to realize that something has gone horribly wrong, and that the story hasn't gone according to his plan after all.[69] He thought that Jesus was dead; he could not have foreseen the Resurrection. We can enjoy a wondrous sense of *schadenfreude* from contemplating the Devil's comeuppance at that moment, his shock at his own downfall.

We humans have been thrown into a dark and broken realm that, for the most part, is under the rule of archons who are hellbent on soular death. But we have not been left defenseless. A hidden weapon has been built into our cores, with instructions to awaken only when the situation seems beyond hopeless. The logic bomb is imperceptible to the system of the world, for it did not come from this world. It has been present in us from the start; it is part and parcel of what it means for us to bear the image of God. Jesus, the Word from before the world, is its herald and activator — and that is part of why He is indeed the Way and Truth

---

[67] John of the Cross, "The Dark Night," *The Collected Works.*
[68] Matthew 27:46; Hesse, *My Belief.*
[69] Girard, *I See Satan Fall like Lightning.*

and Life.[70] He is the open door through which we can overcome the limits of this world, turn around its impending triumph over the living soul.

This world is akin to a grand novel, with God as its author and each of us humans as one of the characters. In this context, the Gospel involves the rather trippy and postmodern gesture of the Author *inserting Himself as a character* into His own novel.[71] That is why we can count on Jesus to tell us the meaning of this dimension we live in. As characters within the grand novel, we can never on our own manage to see the contours of the work as a whole. The story appears as if through a deep and confounding fog — if we even bother considering it at all. The Author, however, has the broader perspective. He knows what the book is about, its major and minor themes, the role of each and every character. To any one of the characters (which is to say, *us*), it might all look like little more than a chaotic soup, a bunch of sound and fury signifying nothing. But through a direct intuition of the Author — which is the essence of the prophetic venture — or via secondhand adherence to the visions of the seers, it becomes possible for us to gain the Author's knowledge of the way things are. This is also why we must speak of *revelation*, or revealed religion. If there is something about this world that can only be known from the standpoint of God, then it follows that we wouldn't be able to know what that was unless He deigned to tell us.

The logic bomb is inherent to the structure of the grand novel; but as such, it is not available to our

---

[70] John 1:1; John 14:6.
[71] Kundera, *The Festival of Insignificance.*

immediate perception as characters within the book. It would be rather reasonable for us to assume that such a thing could not exist, and that the world was very much built with no human meaning in mind.[72] Such is the perspective of "natural" reason, which is a polite means of talking about the normal way the world looks to a man trying to figure things out all by his lonesome. In order for this stalemate to change, we would need to gain the insight of the Author, trust that insight, allow it to transfigure everything. Such a move enables us to rise from natural reason to supernatural intuition — and from that standpoint, the first thing that becomes apparent is that nothing is what it seems.

Jesus died, but still lived; He lost, but still won. This is the original paradox around which all the rest revolves. If we were to formulate it as a law, it would be that the truths of the soul often stand in diametric opposition to the facts of this world — to the point that we must conclude that the world is often set up as a trap to distract us from what is really happening. A man with natural eyes will take a gander at the Gospel, note that its hero was murdered, and conclude that it would be better to not emulate that sad sap. By contrast, a man with soular eyes will see the same scene and conclude that nothing matters more than the project of following Him. The parallax gap is astounding and vast.

When we encounter a story of martyrdom — of a man tossing his mortal life away for the sake of soular truth — do we find it sad, or do we find it inspiring?[73] That is perhaps a good litmus test for whether

---

[72] Camus, *The Myth of Sisyphus*.
[73] Miller, *The Crucible*.

we grasp what's really at stake in the kaleidoscopic book that is this world. Our reaction will depend on whether we still naively think that good people are supposed to win down here in a straightforward manner, or whether we have grown aware of the fact that the truth is more profound and terrible than that. There is indeed a victory ensured for the followers of Jesus and the soular path — but it can only be made out by moonlight, and people who are still blinded by their all-too-natural eyes may altogether miss its trace. They will only see a loser in Jesus and a delusional case in all martyrs. But the man with soular eyes will discern that the logic bomb is ticking, and that the win that matters most has the strange habit of dressing in the drag of defeat.[74] This is what God has in mind, and He is so enamored with this point that He entered His own novel in the flesh to tell us all about it. Perhaps it is an acquired taste, but we must learn to love this game. ❧

---

[74] Horton, "Autofac," *Electric Dreams*.

III 🦋 SEX

SOPHIA'S FOREST

There is something missing from traditional Christian religion; most other worldviews possess a much stronger sexual element. Christianity, however, seems to avoid it almost on purpose — which is odd, given that the religion is about incarnation and *not* purely abstract spirit. Perhaps the early historical Church was anxious to distinguish itself from the surrounding paganism. Relative to the natural worldview of most of humankind, the focus on transcendent spirit was perhaps something of a revolution, introducing a novel dimension of sky that had not yet gained an ascendant influence over human life. But this came at the cost of devaluing the immanent earth — and woman along with it. Such a dynamic is probably at the bottom of certain traditional doctrines that emphasize the masculine element at the expense of the divine feminine, the Woman behind the world. Jesus, for His part, gives no indication of having taken part in this charade. Much the opposite, His attitude toward women was likely seen as radically egalitarian at the time, to the point that even the apostles might have been mortified.[1] A chauvinist impetus may have been at play in tradition's relative negligence

---

[1] John 4:27.

of Magdalene, apostle to the apostles and first witness of the Resurrection. The record painted her a harlot — and maybe she was, although that would only be a poignant and powerful symbol of just what Jesus is here to redeem.[2]

A certain dynamic inherent to loving God could present a challenge for a man: namely, that the Lord Himself is a man. This fact suggests that the way to love Him is different from the way of loving a woman. We love men as brothers, and we love them as heroes. It is a matter of holding in common a purpose and a work, and of honoring great achievement when it's done, with Jesus being the greatest of us all.[3] In a way, we are side by side with each other, and that's how we share a face. The sheer intensity of the love of God might sometimes get mistakenly coded as a sort of romance, even as it moves across a very different frequency. This only seems odd nowadays because we are no longer accustomed to such depths of metaphysical passion.

The love of woman is a rather different thing from the love of God, just as the love of life is different from the love of truth. A man doesn't love life in the same way that he loves God; he loves it in the same way that he loves woman. This explains the paradox that some men who do love truth appear to hate life: the Gnostics of yore very much come to mind as folk of this sort. As a man moves along the soular path, he may come to realize that spirit in and of itself can't give much advice on how to *live*

---

[2] Haskins, *Mary Magdalen.*
[3] Blake, *The Marriage of Heaven and Hell*; Renan, *The Life of Jesus.*

in the very ordinary sense of the word. Rather, the insight of spirit could just leave him paralyzed in the ecstasy of a frozen moment, sending him spiraling off on the course of a less-than-holy fool, bright as an angel but too dull to move from one day to the next.[4] Spirit in itself begins to morph into a kind of poison, leaving the man feeling less alive than undead, as if he is in neither this world nor the other.

Such a juncture is where the Woman enters the picture: her name is Sophia, and this created world we live in is her realm.[5] Pure spirit is not enough; for that amounts to a supremacy of abstract reason over all else, whereas this world is by all indications not a "rational" place. It is more of a lucid dream, with mythologies and ancient legends being more equipped to address its meaning than any logical system of deductions. We are in a sort of forest; and if we try to escape this scenario by sending up a flare, then we would only end up setting the canopy ablaze, turning life into a barren desert. The real project is to turn the forest into the Garden — and this first and foremost requires an *engagement rooted in surrender*. In this realm, the sun of spirit must turn into a soular lamp, so as to not blind and burn everything in the environment. We must find the presence of Sophia within ourselves, and then proceed to accompany her through the forest on the basis of its own rules and parameters. We must use dim lights and soft steps, so that our eyes and rhythms may begin to adjust.

Let us think of this scenario in terms of the Joker from the Tarot, proceeding through encounters with

---

[4] Vodolazkin, *Laurus*.
[5] Mead, *Pistis Sophia*.

all the other archetypes of the major arcana — the Magician, the Empress, the Hermit, the Hanged Man, and so on — all the while plunging deeper and deeper into the mysteries of the soul held by the forest.[6] His soul grows and gains dimension as he acquires not just knowledge, but what has always been meant by *wisdom*: awareness not just of spirit or of flesh, but of their dynamic interplay with each other: the enigma and romance of the human soul. God awaits at the very center of it all — but it is inadequate for a man to attempt a direct connection with pure spirit in the absence of a corresponding alchemical development of his own personality structure. That error is how we get fanatical ideology, narrow dogmatism, and all the rest of the illnesses that follow from an intoxication of indigestible spirit. Guided by the lamp within the heart, we must find our way through Sophia's forest in order to carry on the work of the great redemption: a work that culminates in the holy union of the Woman with the Lord.[7]

THE PYGMALION GAMBIT

The main command of the Stoic philosophy is to never stand in need of anything beyond our own control.[8] The world is seen to be a gargantuan mess that couldn't care less about a man's own desires; therefore, if he wants to achieve peace of mind, he must not invest emotional stock in anything under the world's unsteady jurisdiction. On this account, to have peace is to detach ourselves from the whimsical

---

[6] Nichols, *Jung and Tarot*.
[7] Revelation 19:9.
[8] Hadot, *The Inner Citadel*.

movements of the world and to instead focus on our own souls. This ethos can get pretty extreme: it is sometimes said that a man shouldn't even care what happens to his own family, since he has little control over the fates of others. Needless to say, love is nowhere to be found in this picture. If we love, then we fundamentally attach ourselves to others, make our fates intertwine with theirs. To love is thus a radical vulnerability: it is to place our emotional states at the mercy of forces beyond our own control.

The superiority of the Gospel to earlier visions has everything to do with its radical response to suffering. Whereas Stoicism says that suffering is to be avoided and delivers a game plan for making that happen, the Gospel suggests that to be a true man is to walk straight into the Cross, knowing full well what that entails. We may suppose that a good deal of petty and unproductive suffering can probably be avoided; but our interest here is in the kind that can't — not if a man is to be a living soul and not a block of wood. The problem of investment in the world reaches its zenith when it comes to woman, as even the most soular of men — who have rather little interest in what this world has to offer — likely still do care about intimacy with woman and the prospect of having a future and family with her. It is entirely possible that most of the civilizations that men have built have been for the sake of women, and that most men, left to themselves, would have been more or less content to remain barbarians.

It is difficult to deny that a sort of unholy trinity is in play in the world: money, power, sex.[9] These

---

9 Aurobindo, *The Mother.*

are things to which most men aspire — but the bundle itself is enough to almost push a soular man to despair. To such a man, woman is about communion, the meeting and mixing and melding of hearts. But to this world, woman is more often considered part and parcel of the spoils of "success," with the richest or most powerful guy getting the girl. We may be very partial to romantic narratives of the underdog winning it all in the name of love; of the upstart poet's confessions of passion overpowering the blood diamonds offered by the maharaja.[10] In general, however, life shows us in a most bitter manner that such stories tend not to work out as we hope. Too often, the demonic insight of the behavioral scientists holds sway, and where power goes, there go a lot of women.

From this point of view, the ancient vows of celibacy taken by monks and holy men begin to make more sense. Maybe they were never really about the sex as such. Rather, perhaps they were meant to minimize the temptation of entanglement with the world — the lure to play by its rules, want what it wants — one aspect of which is the desire for woman. The vows could have been a tactic employed by a certain class of men to pursue integrity of soul and detachment from world. But that can't be the final answer. The soul is a woman, which means that for a man to go full soular, he does in fact need communion with woman.[11] But woman is also often tied up with world, and world distracts from soul. This puts a man in a very difficult spot — in particular within our depraved culture, in which soular values

---

[10] Luhrmann, *Moulin Rouge!*
[11] Jung, *Aion.*

have grown less appealing and the crassest sorts of hedonism run rampant without check.

There is one alternative for a man in this position, and it consists of the following: to make like Pygmalion and *build the internal woman*.[12] With such a project, a man could refrain from whoring around and looking for an adequate woman onto whom he can project his own soul. He could instead approach the problem the other way around and work toward achieving a direct communion with the woman who is his heart. From that point, he can project outward, enchanting his entire field of perception — along with the actual women to be found within it.

This move restores a type of self-sufficiency, which is important for practical reasons. It is probably true that women lack interest in weak and needy men, and that they can sense that sort of thing from about a mile away. Yet a man *does* have a metaphysical need for woman, who is soul. Our plan thus provides an avenue through which man can both address his immediate need for woman and not take that need out into the world and display it to all and sundry. The Pygmalion gambit is a way for man to achieve relative autonomy from external need and to then take strength outward, rather than looking at the world with ravenous eyes; a way to focus on what he is able to give rather than what he has to take; a way to pursue, within his own heart, a sacred marriage of moon and sun.[13] This type of charm has the potential to ease much pain and confusion in our broken world, and to produce men who are actually capable of the magic called love.

---

[12] Ovid, *Metamorphoses*.
[13] Chensvold, "Rise of the Warrior Monk," *National Review.*

COSMIC ROMANCE

The Church has had a rather serious problem with the feminine realm. Tradition developed a partial remedy by adopting the veneration of Mother Mary; but when the Woman in her fullness is reduced to *only* the archetype of mother, the results can't help but come across as limited and even a little weird.[14] One example is the notion that Jesus is the second Adam and that His mother is the second Eve. But the first Eve and first Adam were wife and husband — which means that without some strong esoteric elaboration about what exactly Mary is, this whole analogy just reflects a rather bad lack of poetic sensibility. The Gnostics knew more when they spoke of Sophia, the goddess of holy Wisdom. This is the complete Woman, exiled but not dead, whose absence has sent shockwaves of distortion across the ages. It is why the tradition hasn't been able to give a full answer to the question of what woman is — or, for that matter, to produce a positive account of the soular meaning of sex.[15]

In the beginning was Jesus, and He dwelled in Heaven with His consort Sophia. But then Sophia fell away from Jesus, thereby producing the Fall along with reality as we currently know it in this dimension.[16] The cosmic drama thus consists of Jesus and Sophia trying to find each other again and restore the order that once was but is no more; it is about Sophia being to Jesus as Eve was to Adam, before the great divide that got the ball rolling on this

---

[14] Freud, *The Freud Reader*.

[15] Martin, *Sophia in Exile*.

[16] Mead, *Pistis Sophia*.

grand tragicomic thing called life.[17] This is the role of woman in the religion of prophecy, and it has deep roots within the Bible itself. Our narrative helps to explain why the God of the Old Testament seems so angry, even when speaking through the mouths of his prophets, often expressing the precise cadence of a scorned lover. This perhaps comes across best with the prophet Hosea, who was commanded by the Lord to go marry a harlot: as perfect a symbol as there could be for the plight of Sophia in her estrangement from Jesus.[18] The main shift from the Old Testament to the New, then, perhaps consists of this single fact: that God finally managed to find His Woman. The Incarnation suggests the reunion of Sophia and Jesus — tentative for now, but a turning point nonetheless. The Lord shifts from discontent to joyous, much like a lot of men before and after romantic union.

Gnostic lore is good for illuminating some aspects of this mystery; but the great flaw with that vision of the world is in its general rejection of the romance between man and woman, spirit and flesh. From the Gnostic standpoint, the very existence of the body is lamentable — and they likewise have little good to say about the reality of woman, since we are after all brought into the physical world through her. But this is wrong. The Incarnation is a *good* thing, and the Lord is in love with the Woman who lives behind this world. No one here is denying that this world as it stands can indeed be awful. We must observe the difference, however, between rejecting the world

---

[17] Cohen, "The Great Divide," *Book of Longing*.
[18] Hosea 1:2.

versus committing to its transfiguration; calling the world evil versus believing that it could become good with the fullness of time; remaining an eternal bachelor versus redeeming the harlot into a bride.

We could use the metaphor of a ship.[19] If the soul is the sail, then the flesh is the hull. The classic Gnostic impetus is to cultivate an exclusive focus on the sail, to the point that the hull is considered either evil or unreal; the goal, then, would be for the sail to soar off on its own on the winds of God, with no regard for the regrettable weight it left behind. But the truth is that a sail without a hull has no substance, and that a hull without a sail is a shipwreck waiting to happen. The dissociation of the one element from the other is thus a serious problem. What we really want is a *flying ship*, a zeppelin of sorts, to take the entire human person where he needs to go.

Our perspective will of course encounter intense enmity in the midst of our contemporary world. Many today would like to believe that no meaningful difference exists between man and woman, and that gender is just a malleable social construction. We must affirm, however, that there dwells a *poetic* truth to the reality of man and woman, and that this is the ground that we cannot give up. Unpopular an opinion as it has become, this is also why there could never be such a thing as "gay marriage." That statement has nothing to do with the laws of the land, which change like the weather. The point here is metaphysical instead: the nature of the cosmos is such that marriage signifies the union of woman and man, for marriage is

---

[19] Morales, *The Divine Secret of Nothing.*

the mortal symbol of the cosmic romance between Sophia and Jesus. This is the deep reality that can't be changed by whimsy or by will.

Sophia fell out of Heaven and brought all the heavens down with her.[20] Ever since, she has been longing to return home — and this is the exact longing we all feel in our own souls for a greater fullness and transcendence than what we can now know. The Lord was still in Heaven, but He was distraught; for He had lost His soul. And He thus devised a plan to *come down here and get her.* This stratagem began with the Incarnation and went on from there, with Magdalene serving as the human emblem of fallen Sophia within the narrative of the Gospel. And the plan is still in motion: for the Gospel is not just a discrete event, but also a perennial process. It is an archetype that we must all strive to fulfill with the turning of the wheel of every generation. It isn't that Jesus saved Sophia; but rather that Jesus is always saving Sophia, and will continue to do so until the Last Day. The choice is ours to participate in this ongoing cosmic project — and to thereby hasten the end of God's grief and help ring in the reign of enchanted bliss.

THE MISSING LETTER

Male and female genitalia have been made for each other ever since the genesis of animate life. Even *plants* have their own version of this dynamic. We mustn't reduce sex to the simple purpose of material propagation, but we should also acknowledge that the substratum does exist, built into the dimension

---

[20] Mead, *Pistis Sophia.*

we share with all mammals and beyond.[21] So, what shall we make of LGBTQ+ or whatever, an alphabet soup that some rather peculiar folk seem intent on perpetuating to no end? The first two letters are straightforward enough: a woman who is attracted to women, and a man who is likewise attracted to other men. It is a phenomenon that is quite bizarre to the outsider, although it is easy enough to grasp at the level of concept. The B is simple as well, since it is just a mix of the norm and the LG deviants. The concepts get much fuzzier and incoherent from that point onward, although that doesn't seem to bother their ideological advocates in the slightest. Perhaps the confusion itself is part of the point.

Few folk these days seem to really understand why more traditional types think that the alphabet soup is a problem. So, as a man who identifies as old-fashioned (is "O" taken yet?), I will attempt an explanation. Let us be explicit: sodomy involves putting a thing in a hole where it isn't meant to go, a place of decay and waste; and since the entire cosmos is structured in terms of the lifegiving power that only man and woman can generate together, such an act also jars against the music of the spheres above. We do not need to pretend that this stuff is anything other than the perversion it is, even as we swear off disrespect toward people who are driven to engage in such behavior; for we must know that all humans are equal in their dignity before our Maker.

An aviation company trying to get woke once made an advertisement where they had three con-figurations of seatbelts — buckle-buckle, clip-clip,

---

[21] Paz, *The Double Flame.*

buckle-clip — and proceeded to suggest: "It doesn't matter whom you click with."[22] In response, we might suggest that of course it matters, and that we probably shouldn't fly with an airline whose engineers were under the impression that it doesn't. Such jokes aside, the point is that a dynamic of male and female is built into all the realms of reality, whether in the simple sexual function in this world or in the cosmic romance spanning the heavens.[23] Overall, we cannot help but suspect that homosexuality is related to some type of narcissism, being as it is a desire not for the other, but rather merely for a mirror of one's own self. We are likewise obliged to hypothesize that trauma is often behind the original disjunction in the flows of libido.[24]

The transgender dogma is even less in harmony with created reality, lost in phantasms as it is. Sexual differentiation is coded into every cell of our flesh. We are obliged to sympathize with those who feel discontent with the results of that genesis. All the same, to just reject the material dimension in such a literal way would be a recipe for psychosis. If a man wanted to cross-dress and manifest the social role of a woman, then that would probably be just an aesthetic matter, no one else's real business. Nevertheless, the maximalist metaphysical claims of these people present problems that we can't readily ignore, for they deny the ontological essence of sex. Also, the Ts don't believe in sexed bodies — which is to say that they reject the very basis of LGB identity, just in case anyone was still keeping score.

---

[22] Royal Dutch Airlines.
[23] Lewis, *Perelandra*.
[24] Howard, *Chance or the Dance?*.

There is a much deeper problem, though. Even considering only the gays, the "born this way" narrative probably doesn't hold water.[25] A key issue here is that homosexuality is a *behavior*, rooted in desire; and it is very problematic to equate identity with either behavior or desire. For all I know, a man could be gay in the same sense that I have a proclivity to drink too much, and perhaps that is all not such a big deal: we could just be talking about varieties of venial sin. My desire for a beer surely flows from a mysterious place in my nature; and such a desire, if left unchecked, will manifest in discrete behaviors. But would that suggest that my *identity* is D for drunkard? To equate a behavior with an immutable desire, and then to further equate that desire with identity: this is just bad metaphysics. More than that, this whole perspective fails to evaluate whether any given desire of ours is *good*, naively assuming as it does that any desire we find within ourselves is inherently good. Even a rudimentary familiarity with humans should be enough to disabuse anyone of such a notion.

But the worst thing about the Q+ cult has to do with this single fact: they are under the impression that sexuality is the defining feature of what we humans are. This is pseudo-scientific fantasy and an abdication of the truly human destiny.[26] The notion that sex defines a man is one of the more pernicious blasphemies of our late modern world. Wiser men have always known that life is defined by soul, and that sex itself is an ambivalent thing at best. They knew it as a power that could raise us up if our eyes

---

25 Mayer & McHugh, "Sexuality and Gender," *The New Atlantis.*
26 Becker, *The Denial of Death.*

are bright enough, but also more often than not just drag us down into the lowest sorts of mud.[27] To identify whole hog with sex is to believe oneself to be nothing but an animal, which is a sure path to Hell if there ever was one. The sort of man who believes that word and sex, spirit and flesh, were never meant to exist in the sort of schism that they do now — we could call such a man a romantic.[28] To be a romantic is to be a full man: to elevate the beast to the level of the heart, and to compel the angel to descend to that nexus as well. The degenerates who call the shots these days want to leave nothing untouched; but we must know that their infernal brew will be marked, now and forever, by one missing letter: *R for romantic*. The alphabet soup crowd has a very sad notion of what man is, and this identity is the one that they shall always miss.

FORCE OF DIVORCE

There is a sort of love triangle going on in the heavens between the Lord, the Devil, and the Woman. In the beginning, the Lord and the Woman were one; and the Fall first and foremost had to do with a radical alienation in the Lord, through which the Woman grew estranged from Him.[29] We can thus see the project of redemption as a matter of restoring the sacred union. The Devil, however, is the force of divorce, the dark angel who wants to prevent the marriage in Heaven — and to thereby block the redemption of the Creation. He has legions

---

[27] Paz, *The Double Flame & An Erotic Beyond.*
[28] Percy, *The Last Gentleman.*
[29] Blake, "Jerusalem," *Complete Writings.*

of minions, but in principle he is still one; and he is present whenever the rules of this world prevent the fruition of true romance. Is this not, after all, why we are all so fond of stories where the vagrant dreamer ends up duping the wealthy villain and uniting with the woman he loves?[30] Every such narrative is a miniature morality play about the Devil getting his ass handed to him, and of Sophia and Jesus finding their fulfillment in each other.

Looking through this lens, it becomes obvious exactly why late modern feminism is such a godawful ideology: for could there be any honest doubt at this point that it has turned into an agent hellbent on sowing strife between the sexes? It is the rejection of any concept that men and women need each other in a fundamental way. We have come to see such need as a weakness that must be overcome, rather than what it really is: a small mercy offered to us, and a reminder of the possibility of a grand reclamation. Would it be a stretch to suggest that, to late-modern eyes, such dreams matter little when compared against the imperatives of the economy? Capitalism has staged an impressive coup by convincing us that the privilege to sit in a cubicle all the live long day is the epiphany of freedom — and that a woman is not liberated until she enters that jail cell out of her own will. This is not a conversation about the genuine freedom or dignity of women. The point is that today's feminism has utterly turned its back on such concerns, attending instead to endless wars of ideological attrition. Perhaps this sick parody comes full circle with the conquests of the transgender cult, which literally asserts that a man can

---

[30] Cameron, *Titanic*.

be a woman just as well as a woman. Our ancestors may have had their prejudices and problems, to be sure, but we must doubt that they had ever dreamt of a sexism quite that radical.

Furthermore, we are compelled to conclude that alphabet soup ideology is also allied with the Devil, for the precise reason that it seeks to undermine the communion of woman and man. At the archetypical level, homoerotic bonding must seem like a strata-gem deployed by the Devil to bring about a false union between himself and the Lord, disrupting the true project of romance.[31] Literature is replete with examples of this trope, a good one being the story of a vizier who schemes, via outright lies and other creepy machinations, to turn the hero against his bride.[32] And what is life in these times if not stranger than fiction? We may say here, in passing, that people may live as they wish; but it is also true that some of what we all want to do is at least a little regrettable; and a lot of pressure is in place, these days, to not call things by their true names. We must decline to endorse activities and ways of life that undermine our vision of the Light.

It also makes far too much sense that religious faith has become incomprehensible to so many today: for romance is the living image of such faith, and the death of romance must thus also presage the latter's obsolescence. It is the same soular mechanism, which has by now fallen into a state of utter disrepair. We are told that only sad saps fall in love: that it is better to always put oneself first; that we can all

---

[31] Bantock, *The Morning Star*.
[32] Shakespeare, *Othello*.

be anything all the time; and that anyone who tells us different must be a depraved bigot. Then people find themselves standing around and wondering why they are so unhappy with their lives, as they confront the prospect of growing old alone — the gilded cage that they have built themselves. We must acknowledge that this is a rather brilliant infernal trap to ensnare the souls of millions upon millions: for the best way to keep a man in prison is to persuade him that he is free.[33] There is just so much ideological rubbish that must be done away with before it will even become possible for so many of us to consider the Truth again.

The failure of romance could well drive a man to desperation, and the force of divorce can't be separated from the self-destructive impulse that lives in a lot of men. At a certain point of having to deal with the riptide of the lies, we may well opt for a rather radical option: to attempt to kill the hopes that can be killed, so that what is immortal may emerge. As he crosses that juncture, a man might find himself encountering a deity who is searching for His Bride. The man might recognize a trace of himself in that forlorn and yet determined visage, and then give voice the most portentous question of all: "What has happened to us?" And then the Man of Sorrows might begin to speak — to those with ears to hear — about the Devil's devious plan and how to overcome it.

SYZYGY SHIELD

"Syzygy" is one of the most interesting words in the English tongue — a six-letter word with three Ys

---

[33] Huxley, *Brave New World*.

and a Z — and its meaning is even more wondrous than that. The syzygy is the union of complementary opposites, yin-yang style; it is the fusion of the poles that were kept apart from the start; it is man and woman becoming a divine androgyne together, restoring the unity that was lost after the great divide.[34] It is also the ultimate response to the force of divorce. The Devil is banished by the syzygy: no room for him remains in the midst of that union. When the Woman and the Lord are apart, a disturbance emerges in the cosmic field of energy — a pain, a break — and through it, the Devil manages to enter and wreak his signature havoc. With the closure of the gap, harmony is restored, and the Devil has nowhere left to go but the abyss.

I have heard tell of an agent of the Devil who went by an Italian name; he had a single-minded spectral will to prevent the man and the woman of a love story from ever coming together. This is the ending of that legend, spoken in the voice of angels: "A balance has been struck. The lioness and the mercurial scribe have mated, and their passion has set in motion a boundless tumbling tide of awakening. Too late, Frolatti has realized his fatal error. Now he floats in free-fall, and his designs for our endless sleep have been sucked into the firmament. That earthy membrane between your world and ours is slowly dissolving. And in the stillness, the Golden Gate yawns open."[35] This is the sweet cadence of victory, and nothing lifts the heart quite like the sight of romance

---

[34] Cohen, "The Great Divide," *Book of Longing*; Plato, *The Symposium*.
[35] Bantock, *Morning Star*.

triumphant. Every fulfillment of soular romance is a win for the cosmos as a whole, a step onward in the evolution of the world. There is an epic call upon us all. Sin enters the world through each and every individual human heart, and it is also annihilated from the world in the exact same manner. Every win for the living soul is a small restoration of the Kingdom. The syzygy, when activated, then prevents the Devil from setting one toe into the glimmering reality brought into being via — we needn't be embarrassed to say it — the living power of love.

It should be clear enough to us that men left to themselves too often become *free radicals*: they bounce around society like the namesake volatile particles within the human body, unstable and possibly a threat to themselves or others.[36] With the fading of romance, some of the deepest needs of our species do not know where to go to find their rest. We have come to believe that we have evolved ourselves out of our own skin, left behind the entirety of our original inheritance; but our nature becomes no less real as a result of being ignored. Men who would have wanted families might instead become ideological fanatics as they try to give their lives some semblance of the meaning that was promised and then lost. In the absence of the syzygy, we may also find ourselves withdrawing into new recesses of solipsism, trying to court numbness so as to not feel the full brunt of what we lack.[37]

A deep despair resides within the heart of lust. Once the hope of the syzygy has all but receded from conscious awareness, men may feel left with no choice

---

[36] Paglia, *Sexual Personae.*
[37] Murakami, *Men without Women.*

but to just look out for themselves; and this can end in the heinous sin of treating women as transactional *objects*. That is when the Devil can really know that he has scored a critical hit; for the worst of his stratagems is always the sapping of hope. A man may come to think that there is no woman for him; and then he may begin to live in such a way — addiction, violence, depression — that turns this dark thought into a self-fulfilling prophecy. Such a man might soon forget the fact that it is always his prerogative to build the woman of his own soul, falling instead into the no-man's land of illusion and simulacrum.

The original syzygy is the union of Sophia and Jesus, just as the Bible ends with a wedding feast.[38] Since humans are the image of God, we can also take this point to mean that man and woman, together, are meant to restore the Kingdom.[39] The failure of this great venture is the source of more pain and malaise than we dare to comprehend; and the unfortunate truth may well be that the bait of sexual freedom is often to blame for a lot of this fallout. We must be clear: it is difficult to complain about the liberation of pleasure and imagination.[40] But the problem is that faux "freedom" has tossed what used to be a more sanctified domain into the ravenous maw of the free market — with predictably disastrous results, as hedonistic, take-what-you-can-get opportunism distracts us from the project of building a thing of real and enduring value.[41]

---

[38] Revelation 19:9.
[39] Solovyov, *The Meaning of Love*.
[40] Blake, *Complete Writings*.
[41] Houellebecq, *The Elementary Particles*.

When will we remember that cheap sex was never what we dreamt of when we were young, and that we have been sold a false bill of goods by sociopaths who stand to profit from our amnesia? The human soul cries out for the divine union, of which bestial sex, considered in itself, is only a shadow. Everything must begin with a resurrection of the living imagination. Then men and women may once again be able to see each other and themselves for what they are; and the original project, planted in our hearts from the start, may become manifest in the light of full awareness. The Devil doesn't want that to happen, for he knows that this fulfillment would be the end of him. If we want to get going with the final rebellion, then, we must learn how to bring the syzygy shield online again.

THE DARKEST DESIRE

We may observe that from a certain dark standpoint, man is born from woman and thrust into an alien world he can't comprehend that threatens to destroy him at every turn, civilization serving as a precarious bulwark against the omnipresent danger.[42] There is thus a deep reason why man tends to start off at least a little afraid of woman: for if woman is associated with body and Nature, then autonomy of spirit more or less requires man to begin by fighting his way out of woman.[43] Perfect autonomy, however, will always be impossible for man, insofar as to be a part of our incarnate species is to have a dimension of flesh that tethers us to Nature.

---

[42] Paglia, *Sexual Personae.*
[43] Stern, *Flight from Woman.*

Only God has absolute independence; for He created the whole cosmos out of nothing and Himself. A man who craves the total freedom of God thus runs the risk of becoming a solipsist and narcissist. The truth that nothing exists outside of God's mind can become perverted into the false notion that nothing exists outside of a man's *own* mind; likewise, a man could degrade the correct statement that God is at the center of everything into the proposition that everything revolves around his own ego.

Is there any darker of a desire than to want to be God? A wise man once said that the poet must overcome the sadist within himself.[44] To be a sadist is to treat all other beings in the world — and woman in particular — as objects that exist only to be manipulated for the sake of one's own pleasure. It is the desire to become the universal subject, or God, via the reduction of everyone else to the status of mere objects. The poet, world-builder that he is, may have a special susceptibility to this sort of thing, since his eyes already tend to see the world as a source of creative material to be digested by his imagination. But this ethos can go bad quickly; and when it is turned on human beings, the poet becomes a sort of subtle cannibal. In this context, we may also add that the romantic must overcome the fascist within himself. This is the difference between unity as the destruction of the other and the megalomania of the self, versus unity as the loving communion of free selves.

It is certain that a fundamental link exists between sadism on the one hand and the frustration of libido on the other: when life-force can't flow along its

---

[44] Paz, *An Erotic Beyond.*

proper paths to fulfillment, it begins to devour itself and seek escape via darker channels. (In that sense, "kink" is in fact the perfect descriptor, suggesting as it does an unnatural knot in things.) The desire for mutual freedom inverts itself into the desire for control of one over the other, usually man over woman; this dynamic could even get fused with a literal identification of woman with flesh and man with spirit, such that the evil and illegitimate rule of man over woman is conflated with the proper ordering of spirit and flesh. Such submission is sometimes even presented as a picture of the paradisiacal state that existed before Eve was pulled out of Adam, becoming a separate entity who could contradict his desire.[45] It is obvious that this veiled desire for the annihilation of subjective otherness reeks of sadism.[46]

This is not an arcane consideration; rather, the dynamic of sadism permeates today's culture and imagination. We can see it at the political level with the resurgence of the fascist impulse on all ends of the spectrum — always a sign of the desire to engage in a societal play of dominance and submission.[47] But it is also true at a much more intimate and personal level as well. The malady is inherent in the cultural project of normalizing kinks and deconstructing any concept of essential meaning in sex. If the nature of sadism is to treat other humans as objects, then it is all but celebrated in our topsy-turvy times, as the only thing that matters anymore is the magnitude of one's own pleasure, damn any thought for

---

[45] Frye, *Fearful Symmetry*.
[46] Paglia, *Sexual Personae*.
[47] Fromm, *Escape from Freedom*.

the beautiful or the good. It is surely not a coincidence that our culture's entire stance toward Nature
is also sadistic; for how we see Nature will always
be entangled with how we see woman. We seem to
think that Nature is just there for us to *use*, and
that we can therefore get away with assaulting her
for her wealth. Is it any wonder if she then seeks
her revenge? We must wonder where the old-school
ethos of stewardship went, to say nothing of chivalry.

There is no greater enemy of romance than such
a dynamic. Romance is the realization of mutual
subjectivity, the play of entangled freedoms. It has
nothing to do with absorbing all of another's freedom into oneself, or of sacrificing all of one's own
freedom for the hypertrophy of the other's ego. The
natural dynamic of the masculine and the feminine
is not at all the problem. That give and take, reveal
and conceal, is part of the beauty of the world; and
we are obliged to feel pity for folk who fail to see
the charm. The problem is with the degeneration of
the dance into the sad stasis of subject and object,
the betrayal of the impetus to communion. Once we
understand that man and woman are here to help
make each other free, the fantasies that pervade the
late modern consciousness are revealed in their full
demented contours. Some telling metrics, which we
shouldn't deign to name, suggest that a lot of women
dream of submitting to humiliation and becoming
nothing, which is matched by the corresponding male
dream of becoming everything. Where has the original
innocence gone? Its restoration would require all men,
starting with the poets, to renounce the will to power
once and for all — and that means kicking it out of

all our chakras. We must have done with wanting to be God, enact a purification of the heart, accept the soft surrender built into the creatures that we are.

ENCHANTED CHALICE

Our culture has taken to sidestepping the enigma of man and woman. Perhaps this is because the very question of what woman *is* to man has too often been given an inadequate answer across the historical eras, with the domination of women by men being the only response that some stunted souls were able to imagine. The romantic is left asking: what of the poetry? If there were ever a case of tossing out the baby with the bathwater, then this would be it. We must first accept and then see for ourselves that man and woman are made for each other, and that there is a deep and divine reason for this mysterious state of affairs. And if this offends some camps among us today, we may point out how badly *they* offend the romantic temperament.

The issue at hand goes galaxies beyond some crass obsession with the sex act itself. We may consider, for instance, how women often enable men to simply settle down, quell the fevers of their existential angst.[48] This is what one stellar poet has to say about the matter, in a song intended to reflect his wedding vows:

> It's never been my duty to remake the world at large
> Nor is it my intention to sound a battle charge
> 'Cause I love you more than all of that with a love
>   that doesn't bend
> And if there is eternity I'll love you there again[49]

---

[48] Percy, *The Second Coming*; Zmirak, *Walker Percy's Return to the Feminine*.

[49] Dylan, "Wedding Song," *Planet Waves*.

It is inspiring to hear from a man who actually has the power to change the whole world, but also finds that such grand ambitions mean little to him compared to the no less epic project of loving a woman. Much of the storm and stress of our generation surely has a lot to do with the collapse of romance. Although we shouldn't get deterministic about the matter, we may nevertheless observe that great historical cataclysms tend to happen when men are unable to find their natural fulfillment in women: all that pent-up energy must go somewhere, and it often bleeds into wars and dreams of revolution drenched in red. We speak of something more profound than mere sexual frustration. The point is that it is through women that most men grow reconciled with this broken world, and that when the syzygy of man and woman is stalled, pandemonium is often the result — first latent, and then in full form.

There is a sacred woman in the heart of every man, and brute sex can become a perversion of this inherent truth. A lot can be known about a man by how he thinks of woman, since woman is after all his own soul. Pursuing this line of thought, it sooner or later becomes clear that the sexual revolution failed to fulfill its promises: for it has only resulted in a universal degradation of both man and woman, along with the conquest of the intimate sphere by capitalist market logic.[50] A vagina is not just its physical dimension; rather, it is poetically also a chalice, a source of life and water — just as the phallic sword is the symbol of spirit and fire.[51] The physical world

---

[50] Houellebecq, *The Elementary Particles*.
[51] Jung & Franz, *The Grail Legend*.

is a symbol for the world of the soul, and sex is a symbol like others, albeit an unusually powerful one. We thus speak here neither of mere sensual pleasure nor of social politics, but rather of the *poetic* destiny of man and woman as creatures made for each other: two halves of a whole, separated by the Fall and intended for restoration via the praxis of Apocalypse.

The cultural barriers that used to exist regarding promiscuous sex — they were not just there to ruin all our fun. They were, however dimly, reflective of the basic awareness that care must be taken with holy things. What is needed in order to approach the enchanted chalice? What sort of man is *authorized* to do so? Such are the questions that are at the heart of taboos.[52] To go where one does not deserve to go is sacrilege and desecration, and to assume that no such standards exist is the essence of decadence. If the vagina bears poetic resemblance to the temple's inmost sanctuary, then what sort of man should be allowed to enter a particular one?[53] Maybe it should be a man who has shown that he is pure of heart and does indeed love the woman, as opposed to being someone who would just use her up and throw her out with the next week's garbage. There used to be methods through which such matters were ascertained, and they went by old-fashioned names such as *courtship*.[54] These days, unfortunately, we assume that we are too good for such rituals, and that we have dared to go where those before us were too superstitious to venture. If the widespread heartbreak

---

[52] Eliade, *The Sacred and the Profane.*
[53] Howard, *Chance or the Dance?*.
[54] Tolstoy, *Anna Karenina.*

and rage between the sexes is any indication, then our way hasn't worked out so well for us.

The decline of romance is surely connected at the hip with the abolition of enchantment: for what romance teaches a man is that things are not what they seem, and that when his imagination lights up, a transfiguration occurs — first of a woman, and then the whole world. Even the most commonplace things can begin to take on a mythic resonance as we begin to recognize ourselves in the stories of yore.[55] Archetypical forms emerge out of what would otherwise be the most boring of events; a mere trip to the grocery store could come to mean more than much else in this entire realm. This is how the world becomes illuminated, and woman and man are here together to better enable the advent of this magic. When did we see best, and how can we learn to see again? Our world has pulled a grand scam on us, selling us soular death in the name of freedom. If the heathens are happy with that phantasm, then we must leave them be and seek our dream.

CALL OF THE FALL

One of the direst temptations that faces the soular man is to aspire to pure spirit, and to thereby turn away from the whole world of existence, including the Woman behind that world. Such is the obvious impetus behind ascetic codes that prescribe total avoidance of the affairs of the world — including sex, which it is near-impossible to extricate from all of that drama, no matter how "holy" a man may be when left to himself.[56]

---

[55] Bridges, *Urban Cowboy.*
[56] Dostoevsky, *The Idiot*; Cohen, "Hallelujah," *Various Positions.*

Indeed, looking at the decadence of the world as it stands, the instinct of flight is rather reasonable. This is more or less the train of thought that drives the Gnostic rejection of the world; and while it is too fanatic by half, there is still much truth in it, and people who naively reject it as "heresy" might reveal themselves to have too much nostalgia for perfect immanence. It is a sign of soular health to feel at least *some* disgust about having to dwell in this dimension and to suspect that we are foreigners in this land.[57]

To feel a little uncomfortable in this world is the hallmark of the human: for only beasts and lesser lifeforms feel completely at home in this realm, with pure instinct being enough to sustain the flow of phenomena from conception to death. To be human specifically means to have an influx of spirit that prevents such an easy and amoral truce from being able to continue; it means feeling the pain of the break.[58] But that is only the first act of this grand drama. A man may feel aversion to the world, but that reaction doesn't provide an answer; rather, it only raises a fundamental question. We still must know: is that aversion a *good* instinct that should be followed through to the end — or is it instead a point of inflection, indicating the need for a new engagement?

The late-modern answer is that there is nothing wrong with this world, and that anyone who senses such a problem is just ill and should be drugged into happy oblivion.[59] The Gnostic answer is that this world is an illusion and a prison, and that rejecting it

---

[57] John 18:36.
[58] Percy, *Lost in the Cosmos*; Camus, *The Myth of Sisyphus*.
[59] Huxley, *Brave New World*.

altogether is the only path worthy of pursuit. But the Christians have always affirmed that man is both in the world and not of it — and that the actual venture thus has to do with neither the acceptance of the world nor its rejection, but rather its *redemption*.[60] On this point, we register no disagreement whatsoever with the ancient tradition.

Lord Jesus became incarnate, and all of us are obliged to follow suit — which means that the Creation is good, since this is the only realm in which the salvation of the divine marriage can be worked out. To find this place unworthy would then be to reject the human project; it would be akin to acting like a pretentious adolescent who loathes the world for the simple reason that it won't comport itself to his own grandiose self-image. The startling insight emerges that, in a way, *it is better to fall,* since without a fall into the Creation, a man would be neither living nor absent but just more or less undead — an unnatural specter, neither in this world nor of the other. We are thus called to the fall. And this brings us to an ancient and paradoxical notion: the *felix culpa*, the happy fall. Without the Fall, there could be no Redemption, which suggests that in the long run and the big picture, the Fall could well be an unregrettable thing. The painful break must happen before the true and ultimate communion can become manifest, and this epic journey is perhaps much better than never having dared at all.[61]

The movies have much to tell us about this matter. *Take one*: a man must give up his superpowers in order to save the life of a woman he loves. He goes ahead

---

[60] John 17:14-19.
[61] Berdyaev, *The Destiny of Man.*

and makes that bargain, for the woman is worth more to him than his own promised divinity — and via that sacrifice, he becomes an actual god, with a thread of fate that the underworld witches could not cut.[62] *Take two*: a man has abilities that the world could use, but that would also prevent him from being with the woman he loves; and he thus relinquishes them of his own free accord, the rest of this realm be damned. He decides to enter the tunnel.[63] *Take three*: a black-and-white angel falls in love with a woman — and in order to be with her, he decides to literally fall all the way to the ground, at which point he begins to see in full color. He finds the joy he wanted.[64] *Take four*: the Lord comes down here into our world, taking on a human form, making a penultimate sacrifice in order to save His Woman and restore the Kingdom of Heaven. That last one, of course, is not a film at all. It is only reality.

We could think of life as a kind of game designed with certain rules and parameters. Maybe it is like one of those old video games: there's a reptile that has stolen away the princess, and our job is to save her; we'll embark on a process of myriad weird quests; maybe we'll consume some mushrooms on the way (both the good kind and the bad) — and if we screw it up, then we will probably have to do it over and over again, until at long last we manage to get it right and restore the realm.[65] Such is the glory and the plight of our strange species. It is easy to think that the whole game is too ridiculous to even

---

[62] Clements & Musker, *Hercules*.

[63] Lester, *Superman II*; Linidelof, *Watchmen*.

[64] Wenders, *Wings of Desire*.

[65] Miyamoto, *Super Mario World*.

bother, but this is not our way. A man of soul must respond to the call of the Fall, irrespective of how crazy it must look from any "rational" stance — and indeed, he must respond *because* of that.

REDEMPTION'S BELLS

Sophia is the goddess, but a part of Sophia has also fallen: we must hold these thoughts together at the same time, resist the split, embrace the paradox.[66] Sophia is connected with the elements of this world, such as flesh and energy and sex, the natural flow of libido. A fall of Sophia thus implies a fall of what most of us mean by ordinary life — and the redemption of Sophia is thus also the rising of life back to its proper level. And if the Gospel is about anything at all, then of course its theme is resurrection. Jesus is here to raise the dead right here and now, just as He preached of sins forgiven long ago.[67]

One of the most disturbing signs of the decadence of our times is the fact that the sex cult has gone ascendant once again. The alphabet soup stuff is a problem not just because of its various absurd claims, but also because of the more general ethos it represents: the notion that sex is the nexus of identity and the vessel of salvation. If that is how it was, then every dumb animal would be saved, and this fraught human experiment would have all been for naught. The rise of the sex cult strongly suggests a heathen collapse of civilization: we are not growing into a new knowledge, but rather just falling into the old fallacies that follow as soon as we imagine that man is nothing

---

[66] Mead, *Pistis Sophia*.
[67] John 8:11.

but a mere beast. This quest to meet existential problems with sexual solutions is not going to end well.[68]

Part of the issue is that natural sex is tied at the ribs with the pursuit of power. It is about the control and fascination that one person can exert over another; it is about glorying in that egotistical effect; it is about the propagation of the self and the expansion of its influence.[69] This is why a dark nexus exists between woman on the one hand and power on the other: men have always thought about the latter in terms of the sexual access that it could grant them. Such games run all the way across the entire animal kingdom. These are the rules of the fallen world, to which the soular man could only feel aversion. So what does this fact foretell for the project of romance? Being a full human is about raising life from the natural to the supernatural level, just as Jesus raised Lazarus from the dead.[70] It is about knowing that we have a higher call to answer than what has been bestowed upon all other known creatures. It is about alchemical sublimation, through which the raw animal fires that flow through us are refined to a level that is reflective of the true dignity and station due to the bearers of the image of God.[71]

The reign of *ideology* is surely behind many of the problems of these times, the sex cult most of all. Ideology is an abstract system that only exists to delude people away from the realities of their own human condition, like a demented Pied Piper drawing us away

---

[68] Becker, *The Denial of Death.*
[69] Paglia, *Sexual Personae.*
[70] John 11:43-44; Dostoevsky, *Crime and Punishment.*
[71] Paz, *The Double Flame.*

into increasingly spectral realms. With our project here, we seek to develop only a poetic reflection of reality, not any sort of ideology — but of course we will be accused of doing otherwise, though we will not engage with the heathens on this matter. Arguments of this sort are axiomatic and can thus go on forever, degenerating sooner or later into a snake sucking on its own tail. It may be better to share stories instead. I heard tell, for instance, of a debauched and degenerate man who just went to random weddings in order to tell lies to pretty women and sleep with them.[72] It went well for a while — but he finally fell in love with one of them, and then all his fun was wrecked. He could not eat; he could not work; he could not sleep. That was a soular evolution: his heart awakened, and he stopped acting like a jackass.

No more arguments, then. It is better to rest in a Truth as sure as the bells of Easter, which has nothing left to prove and no need of our dialectics or defense.[73] We will simply *declare* by fiat that everything starts to look differently when we begin to see with the eyes of the heart.[74] Do we ever think, for example, about how nice it is to acknowledge when we have done wrong? — to apologize without reservations and to be granted forgiveness? That is a tiny miracle in and of itself. Now that our civilization is in its decadent, gladiatorial, bread-and-circus phase, the dialectic of repentance and forgiveness is confused with weakness. What hope could there be for such a people? Romance entails a similar sort of sensitivity: a willingness to

---

[72] Dobkin, *Wedding Crashers.*
[73] Goethe, *Faust.*
[74] Saint-Exupéry, *The Little Prince.*

step away from all the ego, for the sake of the glory of communion. In poetic terms, the romantic shift could perhaps also be called the *end of the Oedipus complex* — the power-hungry genital fixation that betrays the prerogative of the true and eternal man.[75] It is all about the rising of the heart: not at the expense of all other chakras, but instead its ascendance to its proper throne as the seat of the holy within us humans. We must reverse the original abdication, like the Prodigal Son returning to his home.[76]

And finally, a soular man may begin to understand where his true value lies: not in what he can take or buy, but rather only in what he's able to give and give and give.[77] Such kenosis has always been the law and logic of the living soul. It is perhaps true that we must remain as shrewd as snakes and use discernment in order to refrain from giving to professional takers who will just draw souls dry and make the world a worse place in the meanwhile. Lest we lose our strength and become incapable of doing any further good, such adjustments to this dimension are as unfortunate as they are required. A prophecy, however: unconditional self-giving will turn out to be the most revolutionary thing of all.[78] This is how we grow the ears needed to hear the bells of the final redemption; this is how we rise into our true species birthright; and this is how we help Sophia return to the home where she always belonged. ❦

---

[75] Brown, *Love's Body.*
[76] Luke 15:11-32.
[77] Greenaway, "Through Heaven's Eyes," *The Prince of Egypt.*
[78] Camus, *The Rebel.*

IV ❦ LIFE

THE ECOLOGY OF FLAWS

A lot of insects dwell upon this earth; indeed, the ratio of such species to all other types of life is a rather high one. They often look rather unattractive (to say the least). They don't seem to do much except annoy people, and many of them are even positively harmful. It can be tempting to look at this scene and declare that we should just exterminate them all. Of course, that would be a disastrous proposal; it would have rippling effects that we could not begin to fathom. Insects, like all lifeforms, are part of a grand ecological system, and they fulfill crucial roles within that order. To take an obvious example, some insects are responsible for the pollination of plants — which means that if all the insects were dead, then all those plants would also die. This in turn would affect animals that have relationships with those plants; and this dynamic would work itself all the way up and across the system, possibly triggering a wholesale collapse of the biosphere. It is important, then, to consider the necessity of insects. We may often not like them much, but the startling conclusion emerges that *without the insects, flowers wouldn't exist.*

The human mind is also a system of endless complexity and depth. Every man surely has things that he doesn't quite like about himself, and it is easy enough to make plans to fix them. We could decide that we are going to eat better, work harder, play less; we could commit ourselves to an almost infinite array of stratagems for improvement. Life shows, however, that such things are much easier said than done, and that it is far more challenging than we might imagine to generate any meaningful change. It can feel like five steps forward, four steps back — and that's during the best of times.[1] Something in us appears to resist our own best intentions.

At some level, we might actually like our flaws and not want them to go away; but something deeper is likely also going on. What if there is a hidden factor of which we are not aware? Maybe our flaws are fulfilling an important role within the delicate ecosystem of the mind. We could, for instance, consider the case of a man who drinks too much. He may resolve to do something about that problem, only to find himself back in the same rut time and time again. Considered from the systems perspective, however, what role does booze play in the ecology of the man's own mind? Drinking may catalyze imagination, which is a process of great importance. It may also relieve the lonesomeness of late modern existence, and thereby also fulfill a vital role. The booze itself may be bad, but the booze sparks creativity and communion, which are among the highest of goods. If the man got rid of the habit, then how would the rest of his life look? If he killed his insects, then would his flowers still bloom?

---

[1] Ragan, "Drag My Body," *Exister*.

Efforts at self-improvement could well end in disaster if they do not take the whole picture into account.[2] The personality is a complex system, such that it is difficult if not impossible to alter a single element without affecting all the rest. We may think that we have a flaw, but it is sometimes hard to say whether the thing in question has structural importance within the broader psychic ecology; and if it does, then we would have to think about how to make a change without bringing about a collapse. We may be more ignorant than we think when it comes to understanding the subtle balance through which the holistic personality manages to hang together.

One cynical figure suggests that self-improvement is masturbation; and I suppose that comment is fair enough, in its own way.[3] Then again, it is also true that onanism is identical with itself. So, what if a man's project of self-improvement consisted of trying to refrain from that practice? This looks to be a paradox. Our point is not to say that we should never strive to grow better. First of all, it is outright impossible to live without values, and the attempt to do so could only end in depression — so long as a man isn't too numbed to maintain even a modicum of self-awareness. It is easy to romanticize that sort of nihilism. Done in the best way, it could perhaps even have the cadence of a sort of Zen-esque detachment.[4] But this belies the fact that it takes a lot of work to properly learn how to not care, which itself would be a project pursued with great care. In short, there is

---

[2] Moonface, "Love the House You're in," *Julia with Blue Jeans On.*
[3] Fincher, *Fight Club.*
[4] Coen Brothers, *The Big Lebowski.*

no getting out of the responsibility of our condition.

Moreover, we humans are born to rise to a higher level of being; we are created with this destiny embedded within the deepest caverns of our hearts. The meaning of this life is to be found in the journey toward the holy. The goal is always the pursuit of *theosis* — a greater and greater transparency to the Light from Above, an increasing manifestation of the latent image of God. This is the sort of project that we couldn't escape if we tried: not without abdicating our birthright, killing off the most vital roots of ourselves.

There *is* a sort of "improvement" that we must admit is rather repulsive. When it comes to that, perhaps these words say it all:

> Fitter, happier, more productive
> A pig in a cage on antibiotics[5]

It is misguided when a man attempts to measure improvement by the standards of this fallen realm, and a sense of nihilism in the face of such false idols is a beneficent instinct.[6] However, we should never let this righteous nihilism against false values lead us to a rejection of the true ones as well. The ecology of flaws doesn't mean that we should consign ourselves to dwelling in the mud, blind to the possibility of ever looking up. It only means that we should be more intelligent about the fixes that we want to enact, the beings we want to become — and more forgiving when we mess it all up, as we will. Abstract moral commands sound easy enough, but the mind is too

---

[5] Yorke, "Fitter Happier," *OK Computer*.
[6] Nietzsche, "Twilight of the Idols," *A Nietzsche Compendium*.

complex to brook soundbite answers. There is no way ahead but by experimental process. We must begin with a total acceptance of all that we are — and *then* worry about what, realistically, could be done.

EARLY GRAVE SYNDROME

Too many poets die far too young. There is of course the infamous 27 Club, composed for the most part of rock musicians: Hendrix, Joplin, Cobain. But this is a much broader trend as well. The old Romantics definitely come to mind — Byron, 36; Shelley, 29; Keats, 25. If we are having a cynical day, we could even suggest that Jesus falls into this pattern, perishing as he did at the green age of 33. What is going on here? We could suggest that some people might just have a mission that requires this sort of premature combustion. Maybe the last temptation of Jesus was to imagine Himself to be a normal man, a man who could go on to be happy with a woman such as Magdalene, have children with her, grow old with her.[7] But that was not His destiny. I wonder if poets are also called to walk strange paths, what with their wild call from the soul that can't help but set the priorities of their lives. None of us is Jesus, for He alone took on that destiny; but then again, we are also called to follow Him — which could mean forfeiting our lives early if that turns out to be what's asked of us. And indeed, even the word "early" may be misleading here, for such events just happen in the fullness of time.

There is a practical problem, in any event, which is that too many poets appeal to their creativity to

---

[7] Scorsese, *The Last Temptation of Christ.*

justify their own self-destructiveness. Most often, though, such men end up neither happy nor creative; for their demise was not commanded by the soular call. Maybe it was, instead, just romanticized garden variety sin. We should never *want* to die, and we must make every possible effort to avoid meeting with that fate. Death is what this world does to us, not what we should do to ourselves. Even Jesus did not want to follow through with His grand plan. In the depths of that final night, He prayed that it could be otherwise: "Father, if you are willing, remove this cup from Me; yet, not My will but Yours be done."[8] We must remember always that Jesus did what was needed, but He didn't revel in it. The gospels themselves suggest that He would have chosen an alternative if another road had been open to Him.

We can't pretend to know whether some people are in fact fated by the Lord to not live to a ripe old age. That seems plausible — but we should never lean into such a thought. It will happen if it must; and if it does, then it should be against our wills. This dark mystery is not meant to be taken as an excuse to lead a degenerate life and hasten the end. There is often nothing so fancy as a divine tragedy going on with most of the dying poets; rather, what seems much more probable is that they just don't *dare to be happy.* Some sort of break or trauma is often at the genesis of the creative call, such that poets are often men who aren't familiar with peace. They get used to a state of agitation, start to take it for granted — to the point that if normal joy ever showed up, it might well terrify them. So they decline to get off their

---

[8] Luke 22:42.

medicine, and they wear their misery as a credential signifying their talent.

This is not a good way to be a man, although it is also true that such a path *could* end up producing works of genius. The method of self-destruction is rather akin to the use of physical oil. Many of us suspect that petroleum is unsustainable, and that the long-term future of the world (if it is to have one) will be characterized by the absence of this substance. Yet our society is hooked on oil, which has driven most of the economy and infrastructure of the modern world. Oil has thus done great things for us and continues to do so, even as it can't be sustained and could well end up destroying us if we keep up this habit. We could thus perhaps venture that fossil fuels are to civilization what intoxicants are to the poet.[9] But this analogy cuts both ways, for just as our society will likely have to evolve in its energy infrastructure if it is to survive, so does the poet: society may sooner or later need to shift to solar, just as the poet must learn how to tap into soular.[10]

Fundamental questions emerge, which could be phrased in the following way: what must we sacrifice for the creative life, and at what point is the price no longer worth the while? Does the Lord ever compel us to engage in self-destructive habits, or is that the result of nothing more than the ordinary burdens of sin and neurosis? Such considerations are heightened by the knowledge that, in the long run, an unsustainable mode of life is also detrimental to the creative endeavor. It is not as though our civilization is doing

---

[9] Lycett, *Dylan Thomas: A New Life.*
[10] Rank, *Art and Artist.*

all that well right now; it is all too clear that we are caught in the death spiral of decadence.[11] The same would likely happen to a reckless poet, sooner or later. The imagination itself would begin to atrophy and get sapped, as the days grow shorter and shorter; and it would get to the point that the creativity, which was the alleged justification, also no longer flows.

The ultimate poetic project must consist of learning how to live. The hours of the day must come to resemble the lines of a stanza — and time itself must turn into a medium of manifestation, like the procession of pages in this very book. It is *possible* that the soular call may require us to make some sacrifices, up to and including our very lives. But this is not something that should weigh too heavily on our minds; and it is wrong, at any rate, to use it as a premise to validate all manner of things that would otherwise be altogether unacceptable. We aim at the revelation of the full life — which means that in order to speak the holy word, the poet himself must work to build a holy mode of existence. Failure to do that much would render him little more than an extravagant hypocrite. The word must turn flesh, the idea become incarnate. It is not enough for the beauty we believe in to dwell in the mere ether, removed from the everyday mush. The Light from Above must permeate everything, and we must *carve* it into place via the medium of our own carnal existence.

A WISE SACRIFICE

A signature malaise of our times is that we believe we can have it all, and we insist on keeping all options

---

[11] Barzun, *From Dawn to Decadence.*

open.[12] But this posture is unreasonable and adolescent (in the negative sense of those words). When we are young, the whole world may seem wide open to us. A child has much room for development, and there is a huge scope of possibilities as to what he may or may not become. As we get older, however, we acquire a past and invest in certain parts of ourselves, at the necessary expense of other aspects. To do one thing at a given moment is to *not* do all the other things that could have been done in that same moment; and by performing that specific action, we incline ourselves closer toward one path and farther away from all the alternatives. We thus see an inevitable exclusion, a narrowing down of choice based on our past decisions and current state.

A man who insists on keeping all possibilities open is like a writer who produces only the first page of a hundred different books: that could be an interesting experiment, to be sure, but the cumulative effort would amount to just about nil. The classic adolescent malady is to defer the incarnation and continually dwell in a realm of pure fantasy and potential.[13] It is good to have imagination, of course — but the problem is that Truth is in life, and life must be lived in the actual world. To never bother *entering* the latter arena is thus to cut oneself off from the start from the possibility of salvation, just as the freedom of the solipsist turns out to be nothing but a glorified prison.[14]

A good example of this dynamic may be found in the situation of a man who will not cheat on a woman.

---

[12] Bauman, *Liquid Love.*
[13] Kundera, *Life Is Elsewhere.*
[14] Kierkegaard, *The Sickness unto Death.*

There are surely some experiences to which that man would not have access. While he is in a relationship, for example, he cannot try to find another woman on the side for the sake of some excitement. From the standpoint of an amoral womanizer, this committed man (let's call him a romantic) must seem like a bit of a sap, given all the apparent opportunity that he is passing up, and all in the name of such old-fashioned scruples. But that's not it. That's not it at all. Some experiences can *only* be had once certain conditions have been met. A relationship establishes the context for the development of a greater understanding and intimacy and trust; and when the romantic chooses not to cheat, it is because he wants to manifest *those* possibilities, which could not be accessed in any other way. The womanizer, on the other hand, has access to endless random stimuli, but he forfeits the option of delving deeper into the communion.

We could suggest that the romantic sacrifices breadth for depth, whereas the womanizer chooses breadth at the expense of depth. Is it better to write one book, or to write only the first page of a hundred books? Either way, a sacrifice must be made, and it is delusional to believe that we could have it all at once. There exists a crucial potential that the shallow man must always miss, by simple virtue (or, rather, vice) of being what he is. All else being equal, we may permit ourselves to say that depth is better than breadth. Indeed, accessing the bottom of all depth — where God lives with His elixir of immortality — is a workable definition of the very objective of this human condition.[15] To drift around

---

[15] Nichols, *Jung and Tarot.*

on the surface of things is to not really live at all; and the longer a man pursues that modus operandi, the sadder he becomes. What is needed is a *promise*, a commitment, that can dispel the relativity of this whole charade and generate a new reality via pure fiat of soular will.

As it is with a woman, so also it is with the Lord: fidelity produces new possibilities that would not have been available had the covenant not been made. This is also how we should think about the old-school notion of "wrestling with the flesh," which is a matter of not sexual repression, but rather alchemical sublimation.[16] So long as a man is controlled by his own selfish desires and egotism, he will see the whole world in terms of his own need, and that need will serve as a distorting funhouse prism that prevents him from ever accessing the true communion. A general principle is in play here, and it has to do with the sacrifice of the lesser for the greater. Just as the only way to access the intimacy of romance is to forswear the illusion of adventure, the only way to maintain fidelity to the Lord is to reject the pathetic thrills of false idols. A man is called to give up loveless sex and the worship of golden animals in order to gain access to the heart of the woman and the Light from Above. But it is clear that such limits are the very contours of such a man's freedom: this is how he becomes able to do what he wants.

Martyrdom it also not what it seems. It is just a matter of a man sacrificing the lesser for the greater, although it has to look outright bananas to folk who

---

[16] Deleuze & Guattari, "How to Become a Body without Organs?," *A Thousand Plateaus*.

can't begin to comprehend what such a man is playing at: namely, the integrity of the immortal soul.[17] We must understand that there always exists what may be called a soular opportunity cost. To pursue one avenue is to reject all others; and, as time passes, this decision tree grows and grows — at some point, we find that we have turned ourselves into the men and women we are, for better or for worse. Wisdom must consist of becoming as aware of this unfolding process as we can, and the sooner the better. Then we could gain some modicum of governance over the dynamic, lead it with the compass of our own deepest values and desires. This is human freedom, and there is no other.

AURAL HYGIENE

Everything wants our attention, and entire industries are built on nothing but the seduction of our eyeballs. This dynamic also has predictably unfortunate effects on the quality of what is made. It is a cliché by now to point out that journalism has become a failed profession — and to a large extent, that is because of what the profit motive does to integrity. If we accept the basic premise that what most people find *interesting* is not the same as what is good or important, the implications follow as a matter of course. We are all asked to whore ourselves out on the airwaves, treating our own selves as personal brands that stand in need of cultivation and sale; and in the process, we have forgotten the ancient wisdom that proclaims: "Beautiful things don't ask

---

[17] Plato, "Crito," *Five Dialogues.*

for attention."[18] It goes without saying that our world can't comprehend such a sentiment.

It remains true that we are what we eat — and, if anything, this must be even more true within the domain of the imagination than the realm of the flesh. The information and knowledge that we absorb from our experiences play such a huge role in the formation of our very ideas of what we are. We humans are creatures of dialogue, and it is only through engagement with the *other* that we begin to develop a sense of ourselves.[19] The nature of the other is thus also crucial, since the other becomes a part of us. In this context, few things are more depressing than a quick perusal of the trash that has managed to capture our collective attention. Pornography, for instance, is omnipresent, and as popular as one might expect. Then there are people always getting worked up about the political gossip of the day: gossip that we know will be forgotten by the time the moon changes phase — although that does nothing to mitigate the vacuous passionate intensity. So perhaps we should refrain from mentioning what "tweets" — a parody of birdsong — have done to our collective attention span. Old-fashioned friendship also looks to be in recession, as folk flock to social media to get the quick endorphin fix of validation, delivered by the click of a button.

We must practice *aural hygiene* and take care about what we absorb. This is not about mere fragility, or the inability to deal with the world without getting overwhelmed. Rather, it is a matter of the awareness

---

[18] Stiller, *The Secret Life of Walter Mitty.*
[19] Buber, *I and Thou.*

that we make a decision with every perception, and that to pay attention to the lesser is most often to cut ourselves off from the possibility of accessing the greater. We should be mindful of rabbit holes, for not all of them are as fun as the one that Alice went down.[20] The discourse of the day and age has a way of imposing severe limiters on what we are even able to imagine. The scope of what human life could be is just so *vast*, encompassing all of what has ever been and potentially much that we have thus far only dreamt of in our wildest imaginings; but so long as we let the current order of dimwits control the parameters of our thought, we never consider more than a sliver of that grand trust, dulled and numbed as we are by the continuous delusional barrage of this shadow show that masquerades as the real.[21]

Consciousness is developed through engagement with the world. We should perhaps think more deeply about what we do with our *hands*, which are crucial exactly because we use them to touch and build things in the world. (Maybe this is also part of why elephants are so marvelous and may well have some sort of internal life: they have their trunks, which function very much like hands, opposable thumbs and all.)[22] More than that, while we have our hands and flesh and five senses, we should never forget that we only have one organ of perception — which is the imagination, an active and living entity. The imagination is a sort of hybrid of hands and stomach: it reaches out and grasps things in the world, and then

---

[20] Carroll, *Alice's Adventures in Wonderland.*
[21] Plato, *The Republic.*
[22] Keiper, "Do Elephants Have Souls?," *The New Atlantis.*

it also digests them in order to constitute itself. All our senses are open windows, and the imagination is the true seer who lives within the house. But as the poet says:

> This Lifes dim Windows of the Soul
> Distorts the Heavens from Pole to Pole
> And leads you to Believe a Lie
> When you see with not thro the Eye
> That was born in a night to perish in a night
> When the Soul slept in beams of Light.[23]

If the eye is only a lens, then what dwells behind it, and who directs its gaze? Such a question has the power to throw us back upon ourselves, lead us to a quiet place — familiar despite its strangeness.

As we get into the groove of practicing aural hygiene, we come to realize the forgotten insight that the destiny of the imagination is to become an active agent rather than a passive screen. The ironically named era of the "Enlightenment" taught us the lie that the mind is but a blank slate upon which the images of the world are projected, and that we are but spectators of what is beamed to us. Nothing could be farther from the truth. The imagination creates its reality — and the greater the integrity of the imagination in question, the greater the reality. We must break out of our culture's hypnosis in order to reclaim this primordial prerogative. Toward that end, we must also reject the soular inputs that do nothing but drag us down, insisting instead that everything that crosses into the palaces of our minds be worthy of entering those enchanted courts. We should vow to tell

---

[23] Blake, "The Everlasting Gospel," *Complete Writings.*

all aspiring stimuli to remove their shoes before they come in: for they will be standing on holy ground.[24]

THE ALLURE OF PATTERNS

Our brains are quite excellent at pattern recognition: we look around our environments and discern all sorts of connections between things that may at first glance seem separate from each other. Some may chalk it all up to a survival advantage associated with this skill. For example, people who could detect threats around them in the forest or wilderness were surely less likely to get killed. But we may also posit that pattern recognition has a great deal to do with the creation of *meaning*, which is no less essential to human survival. What is a great novel, anyway, but a vast constellation of meanings, distilled to a level of bootleg potency that can seldom be found in the "real" world, due to all of the static and white noise mucking up our senses?[25]

It is difficult to ever discern the meaning of any one object or event all by itself. Rather, meanings emerge from a system of relations, as they refract off each other and become amplified in the process. The meanings begin to coalesce into a thematic *narrative*; the story then tells us about the nature of the world we live in, along with the value and valence of our own roles within it. A higher density of connections produces a greater sense of meaning; and the brighter a man is, the greater the level of density he may be able to generate, pulling together meanings where others may well see nothing.

---

[24] Exodus 3:5.
[25] Tolstoy, *Anna Karenina*.

A dark side also exists to this process, however. Sometimes, a man could begin to see meanings that are quite simply not there. The meanings may haunt his own head, but they would have no objective correlate in the created world. A man may believe, for instance, that he is at the center of a spy conspiracy and that he is getting coded messages in every newspaper — when in fact nothing of the sort is happening.[26] A high degree of cognitive processing power would be required to fall into this sort of snare; for many people might just not have the capacity to generate such intricate narratives within their own minds in the first place, delusional or otherwise. Thus, a man who begins to tap into the vast power of pattern recognition could well be on the precipice of something huge; but it may also not be clear whether the dynamic will resolve itself into creativity or madness.

A man could come to believe that the advertisements on every passing bus on the city streets are specifically trying to tell him something. At one level, this is of course wrong, since the whole cosmos is not centered around the man, and the busses do not exist for his own sake. To believe otherwise at this juncture would be nothing but simple narcissism. Yet there is a greater complexity going on. Every man truly *is* at the center of his own field of perception; and it is also true that from this subjective standpoint, the entire world *is* an infinite fountain of meaning, with every last thing serving as a potential vehicle through which the Lord tries to speak with us. At this level, a man is thus *not* wrong to believe

---

[26] Howard, *A Beautiful Mind.*

that the ads on the bus are speaking to him, along with anything else; and the problem would be not with him, but rather with the people who lack the requisite intensity of imagination to see the meaning that everywhere shines forth.

There is still an open question, though, and it has to do with this single point: what is the difference between poetry and psychosis? Poetry is the project of enchanting the world and producing maximal meaning; psychosis is the result of attempting to do so but meeting with failure, growing hopelessly lost instead within the labyrinths of one's own twisted head. It is a rather fine line between the one and the other. Appeals to social norms will be of no avail; for the poet and the psychotic are *both* outside of such norms — the one above, the other below. One good criterion for discernment may be whether the meaning that is produced is one of terror or of wonder. The hallmark of a paranoiac pattern is that it leads to a man feeling more and more persecuted as the meaning grows denser — and he ultimately grows incapable of trusting anyone at all, much less engaging in genuine soular communion. By contrast, a poetic pattern serves to make life richer and richer, adding increasing layers of beauty and resonance to the stuff that is there — until the veil that separates this world from the other achieves a state of near-total translucence, and everything becomes ensconced in the meaning bestowed by the Light from Above.[27]

But even this criterion is a little complicated, since there could well exist a genuine pattern in the world that is rather ugly. The prophets of the Old Testament

---

[27] O'Siadhail, *The Five Quintets.*

surely discerned dark truths about the nation of Israel and foretold of doom and gloom unless the people changed their ways.[28] Their visions did not necessarily produce beauty, but they were nevertheless tuned into a deeper reality. A pattern of terror is bad; at the same time, terror is also how heathens experience the Lord, and in a sense that experience is good. Could a glorious epiphany at the personal level translate into a vision of great horror when turned toward the world? Maybe it is a revealed reality, or maybe it is just the manifestation of a man's own obsessions and neuroses. It is probably precarious to make any serious comment on this matter in terms too broad; for a lot depends on the discernment of the Holy Ghost, along with retrospective confirmation. Another way to say it is that the judgment of prophecy versus paranoia is often a matter of *trust*, which can't really be evaluated outside of specific situations or relationships. Perhaps the most a man can do is speak his own vision of beauty and truth, call out whatever in this world appears as its enemy — and then just pray and hope for the best. Such may be the station of us humans.

IMAGINAL EXTINCTION

Our thoughts begin to shift when we begin to wonder who made us, and what for. The default notion in our world is that we humans are creatures built for infinite self-invention, with every limit (of ethics, of gender, of whatever) being little more than an offense against what's assumed to be our primordial freedom. But is that really how it is, or is this belief tantamount to a psychotic delusion, produced

---

[28] Isaiah 8:14; Jeremiah 6:2.

by a civilization that is bound to eventually destroy itself?[29] We should at least consider the possibility that we were created with certain parameters in mind — and from that point, we may also wonder whether human sexuality, like everything else about us, is intended for one thing or another. This is just a narrow version of the bigger question: namely, whether human life itself has a meaning and intent aside from that we deign to give it.

In every other realm but sex, people seem to understand that what we find pleasurable is often not the same as what we should know to be good. Most of us know that we shouldn't eat pie every day just because the prospect of it can tantalize; and we also tend to understand that we shouldn't shoot up heroin, although by most accounts the high is fantastic. When it comes to the specific topic of sex, we somehow imagine that whatever we want is good by definition. More than that, people turn their particular perversions into identity badges, declaring that *this* one thing is what they are above all else. Two main premises, however, can assist with clearing up the late modern confusion in this area. The first is that sex was made for woman and man, in harmony with the cosmic romance; and the second is that sex was meant to be relational — a mode of communion. If we just keep our eyes on these basic parameters, then a lot of the fog of our decadent culture begins to disperse. The first premise, for its part, makes short work of the entire alphabet soup cult.

The second draws us into a realm that affects almost everyone today, touching as it does on the

---

[29] Bauman, *Liquid Modernity*.

matters of pornography and masturbation. Christian
tradition has long insisted that these things are just
no good; but over time, people have clearly forgotten
why that is so, assuming instead that all the stigmas
are here for no other reason than to just stifle our
enjoyment of life. We must awaken the original wisdom of the soul, which sometimes involves excavating
the truths that are no longer recognized beneath
their harsh and dogmatic shells. Okay, then: one of
the problems with pornography is simply that those
are actual women in those images and films — women
with souls and lives all of their own. But the man
viewing the content has no real relations with them,
and the women become simulacra upon which he can
project the phantasms of his own haunted head. This
point leads into the main issue, which is that porn is
an abstracted *specter*. As such, it awakens a different
response in a man's soul from what happens in an
actual engagement with a flesh-and-blood woman.
Porn is a delusion, and the more a man looks, the
deeper he sinks into the quicksand of his own solipsism. It is a good day for a man when he finds the
prospect of porn just boring; and it is an even better
one when it makes him want to get sick.

An element of complexity nevertheless remains
in play, and it mainly has to do with the inherent
beauty of the female form, which has been a subject
of fascination since the early days of our species. It
seems difficult to deny that certain kinds of erotica
have genuine aesthetic value.[30] Indeed, it can feel
rather tempting to sink perception into the warm
bath of woman's gorgeous image, balance the flesh.

---

[30] Paglia, *Sexual Personae*.

But that can then lead to a rather predictable problem, and we thus have no choice but to now take up the issue of masturbation — perhaps one of the most misunderstood of the ancient bans. The generic view in our world is that there could not possibly be anything wrong with it. However, if human sexuality is intended as a vessel of communion, then the practice constitutes a betrayal of that sacred trust and a regress into spectral headspace; it is reflective of a man seeking a false completion all on his own.[31] We all know what it means when we suggest that a man is engaged in *intellectual* masturbation; and no one in his right mind would consider it a compliment. Is it not absurd, then, that the same vague shame over futility and waste is no longer felt about the literal act that gave rise to the figure of speech?

The cards seem to suggest that this problem will only grow worse over time. Virtual reality is imminent, and we can all guess what one of its first uses will be. Artificial intelligence is also right around the corner — and it requires not a twisted imagination, but rather just common sense, to understand that AI will find its way into synthetic sex dolls in short order. Once this snowball from Hell gets rolling, it will be almost impossible to stop, given the culture's evisceration of the requisite moral language for us to even attempt any lucid thought on this topic. These machines are trying to drive us extinct, and we may no longer have the resources to resist.[32] Scanning across this dark sky, "the abolition of man" is the only meaningful phrase that comes to mind: men without

---

[31] Howard, *Chance or the Dance?*.
[32] Kingsnorth, "The Basilisk," *Emergence Magazine*.

chests, steadily degrading into some horrendous chimeric union between a swollen head and a priapic third leg; men whose actual life energies have been cut off from their rightful flows and invested into amorphous specters instead.[33] Behold, for this is where our "free" choices have led us. I am tempted to ask if we are having fun yet — but the grotesque fact is that many among us would probably say *yes*.[34] Perhaps a clown will emerge upon a stage and yell that the theater is on fire, only to be met with unbelieving jeers from an audience who thinks that the warning is just a part of the performance: and thus might we continue with our inverse pilgrimage into the abyss.[35]

THE DROWNING MAN

A huge trap is built into our modern concept of compassion. We should always feel sympathy for the pain of others, to be sure, and our ideal would be for no one to ever have to hurt again. But it is also true that a lot of people just bring their own problems on themselves — and, more than that, they are toxic enough to want nothing more than to drag everyone else down into their own black holes. There are times when we might think that we are being nice; whereas what we are really doing is handing ourselves over to a quicksand sacrifice. When dealing with a demon, we can hope to resist the dark influence and continue in one piece with full integrity intact. But trying to *save* the demon? — are we feeling quite that reckless?

It is of extraordinary importance to understand

---

[33] Lewis, *The Abolition of Man*; Percy, *The Last Gentleman*.
[34] Hoeullebecq, *The Elementary Particles*.
[35] Kierkegaard, *Either/Or, Part I*.

that even the Lord can't save those who don't want
the grace. This is part and parcel of the double-
edged gift of spiritual liberty. Jesus was able to drive
demons out of people only when they begged Him
to do so; He could perform miracles only when the
recipients believed and had faith. The Lord does not
work such magic against an unwilling audience; for
that would be against His very character. He may thus
sometimes seem cruel — but this is only a matter of
perspective. His general *modus operandi* is to let us
humans destroy ourselves until we have had enough
and come around to seek Him again. Respect for true
freedom prohibits any other way.[36] We humans can
always choose to continue on our infernal paths, and
the Lord will not do a single thing about that. He
can only hold His bastion and let us suffer — until
we hit a rock bottom that might persuade us to seek
the better way.[37]

At a very human level, it can be so hard to come
to terms with the awareness that we cannot save others. The better among us sometimes fall into abusive
relationships as a result. We may think that our loved
ones could be saved, somehow, if only we stayed true
and loyal enough; if only we held the light and set the
good example. But they often just take and take until
there isn't much left of us, and we end up needing
to bail for the sake of basic survival. We develop a
messiah complex, attempting work that is far above
our pay grade and failing to have adequate faith. We
must come to know that only the Holy Ghost holds
the power to save others, and that such work must

---

[36] Berdyaev, *Dostoevsky: An Interpretation*.
[37] Cohen, "It Seemed the Better Way," *You Want It Darker*.

be left to Him. There are men and women among us
who would weaponize our compassion, turn it against
us in a narcissistic bid for control and dominance.
It is easy for an empathetic person to fall for them,
insofar as one fails to realize that such a dynamic is
a sick caricature of self-sacrificial love.

Some people are as a drowning man who splashes
all over the place, making a big ruckus, while expect-
ing someone to jump in and save him.[38] All his fuss
will probably ensure that, if an intrepid would-be
rescuer does attempt it, they are both going to perish.
Worse than that, he might actually *want* to drown,
and he might just be seeking some excuse to take
someone else down to the ancient locker with him.
We may also observe that insofar as a man hasn't
dealt with his own demons, he will never be able to
help but externalize them onto others.[39] He will talk
about nothing but himself and his own concerns; he
will see nothing but the inside of his own forsaken
head; he will do nothing but invite others to participate in his downward spiral. Such a man can only
be a venomous influence on everyone around him.
As people grow aware of this fact, they will begin
to practice avoidance — and he, in his radical self-
absorption, will think of this as another offense done
against him: for in his own eyes, he could never be
anything but the victim.

We can forgive people who have done us wrong
whenever we want, but we should also understand
that forgiveness has two very different modes: there

---

[38] Bob-Waksberg, "The View from Halfway Down," *BoJack
Horseman*.
[39] Jung, *Aion*.

is the cup, and there is the sword. Most folk think of
forgiveness as the feminine cup. This has to do with
the restoration of relations, the return of a status quo,
the inclusion of the drowning man into the system
that was before. Such a notion is compassionate, and
it tends to give us warm feelings — but we may well
forget all about how by extending the communion
chalice in so promiscuous a manner, we might be
enabling the abuser. The Gospel is about gentleness,
to be sure, but it possesses a hidden sharper edge as
well; and from that clear sky, forgiveness could well
take the form of the masculine sword. This signifies
the annihilation of relations, a justice that trumps
all soft pieties. It is the awareness that sentimental
people are often the most cruel ones around, what
with their ersatz emotions and incapacity for actual
empathy; it is the knowledge that we must take care
of ourselves if we are to have the strength to ever be
a rock for anyone else.[40] Do we have the courage to
drop the sword, let the drowning man go, leave the
dynamic of repentance and salvation in the hands
of the Ghost?

As a closing note, let us not forget the importance of *boundaries*. We could perhaps say to ourselves: "I am not anyone else, and no one is me — and,
moreover, I am not Jesus; for only Jesus is Jesus."
Not ours is the saving power of the Ghost to send
or withhold. We should consider ourselves as mere
lighthouse keepers, holding what beauty we know
and hoping that it could give guidance to lost and
struggling souls. Their fates are not our prerogative,
and what will happen to them will happen as it must,

---

[40] Kundera, *The Unbearable Lightness of Being*.

irrespective of our own best intentions. We must turn away, keep the undead wolves at bay, and refrain from trying to be too cool and attempting what only the Lord Himself could do.

SIN AND ANTINOMIANISM

Antinomianism is the belief that grace releases a man from his obligations to the moral law; that when a man is saved, he is immune to sin. At one level, this is obviously true: to have one's heart turned is indeed to have it turned away from sin — which means that insofar as a man dwells within a state of grace, he is incapable of sin. The doctrine itself, though, is most often taken in another direction. A man declares that he has been saved, and that therefore *anything he does*, by definition, can't be a sin. The idea would be that people can lie and cheat and harm and kill; but if they have been saved, then these things wouldn't disqualify them from the state of grace. It is easy to see how this whole line of thought could go horribly wrong. Among other things, such antinomians reject Jesus's most basic criterion that by our fruits shall we be known.[41] There is indeed such a thing as evil; and to be saved is to have a constitutional aversion to it; and no level of internal illumination could "liberate" a man to commit evil while still remaining in a state of grace.

With that disclaimer having been expressed, a deep truth nonetheless exists within the antinomian view of things. The moral law, for the most part, is a blunt instrument. It provides guidelines — most of them negative ("thou shalt not") — at a very high level of

---

41 Matthew 7:20.

abstraction, such that when it comes to situational application, the results often range from the absurd to the cruel. We have the obvious Robin Hood example, where stealing is bad in general, but stealing from a tyrant in order to feed the poor may well be good. Likewise, when Jesus came to this world, the laws of Hebrew society found Him to be bad — so bad that He had to be killed like a common criminal. But we know that Jesus is the Lamp of the world, the fullest epiphany of all that is good. Something strange is thus going on, and it has to do with the fact that what any fallen society or culture considers good may be a highly watered-down version of what is truly good in the Kingdom of Heaven, or even a total corruption of it altogether.[42]

There is still much that is in fact good in common morals.[43] Most societies, for example, have statutes against wanton killing — and nothing about our vision could abrogate the adherence to such a precept. There is no such thing as "beyond" good and evil here, and to disregard the commandment against murder is simply to fall into evil. The dividing line is thus not between what society endorses and what it doesn't. Rather, we must evaluate *everything* from a higher standpoint, validating the places where society and its laws are correct and rejecting the places where they are not. Society is always pharisaic, having laws but not grasping their inner spirit. It may have a law against murder, but it does not understand exactly *why* murder is so terrible. Society still accepts numerous ways of killing people, including culpable callousness

---

[42] Berdyaev, *The Destiny of Man.*
[43] Frye, *Fearful Symmetry.*

in the homeland and barbaric misadventures abroad. But the prophet perceives that all humans dwell in one grand form, Adam Kadmon, and that murder, as the ultimate repudiation of this reality, amounts to sticking a knife into the divine fabric of everything. Society grasps in the fog for things it does not comprehend, drawing spectral abstractions from what was once a living poetic vision.

It may sometimes become necessary for the prophet to break the false law in order to pursue the true one, engage in outlaw actions that violate the letter in order to honor the spirit.[44] We thus have a *relative* antinomianism on our hands, through which the prophet is liberated from obeying moral strictures that are beneath him and that in fact impede the full flowering of the living soul. But we must also see that there is no such thing as an *absolute* antinomianism — at least, not one that could in any way be distinguished from narcissism and nihilism. Every man is answerable to someone, and a man who says that anything he does is good by definition is a victim of severe soular illness.[45]

This point becomes particularly acute when we consider the situation of the artist. Many great artists have been notorious for being pretty awful in their actual lives and relationships with others, and they have often justified this behavior by way of appeal to their creative impetus.[46] At best, such a tradeoff is a Faustian venture: a deal with the Devil, a sale of one's

---

[44] Thoreau, *Civil Disobedience*.

[45] Dylan, "Gotta Serve Somebody," *Slow Train Coming*.

[46] Polikoff, *In the Image of Orpheus*; Max, *Every Love Story is a Ghost Story*.

soul for the sake of vital power.[47] This mechanism of compensation could well lead to the production of great art; but if our main concern is for the human soul, then we must wonder at what cost.[48] It may be better to just be a good man instead.

The artist may sense the impulse to make excuses for his failures and sins with the thought that his imagination puts him above the law; he may imagine that his albatross wings excuse his problems with walking.[49] He may believe that the ecology of his flaws is in acceptable ramshackle order, and that he should not bother embarking on any potentially counterproductive projects of self-improvement.[50] This is a complex subject, more difficult than it looks. The work of the artist is certainly independent from the artist himself, and no work should be condemned because of heinous revelations that emerge about the life of its creator. We must admit that this stance could have the perverse effect of incentivizing bad behavior, since the artist could still tell himself that his depravity was worth it. Who knows? — perhaps sometimes it was; the Lord can judge. The main thought that we should keep front and center is that the stakes of this game are nothing less than our own immortal souls. A man may be willing to part with that most valuable of all pearls; but if he is as elevated as he thinks he is, then he would probably think again and back away from the cliff instead of going through with that infernal wager.

---

[47] Goethe, *Faust.*
[48] Rank, *Art and Artist.*
[49] Baudelaire, "The Albatross," *The Flowers of Evil.*
[50] Moonface, "Love the House You're in," *Julia with Blue Jeans On.*

THE ROYAL NOVEL

All of existence is a royal novel, composed by the Lord Himself, and we humans can understand ourselves as characters within that kaleidoscopic narrative. How were we made, and what do we want to become? These are the central inquiries of the only sort of *ethics* that we find still worthy of the name. Any person is a substantial amount of mass drifting through what we know as spacetime. It takes a substantial amount of force to move this sack of flesh across this dimension, but most often it seems to happen of its own accord, with no conscious input whatsoever. We must thus wonder: where is this flesh moving, and is it doing what we want? There could be a lot of power in achieving conscious mastery of all that kinetic energy. Do I want to play *this* song on my electronic device? Do I want to put *this* food into my physical apparatus? Do I want to spend my evening in *this* bar (or, indeed, any such establishment at all)? Decisions are continually going on, and every single one of them forms us into the characters that we become. There is an incredible amount of energy flowing through our flesh at every single nanosecond, and a lot could happen if we gained awareness of it all. The original magic has to do with bending the electricity that flows through our own nervous systems, altering the grooves to enable a freer and fuller incarnation of spirit.[51]

We could say that an aesthetics of personality is at play, where the most important question of all has to do with *character development* within the novel in

---

[51] Konietzko & DiMartino, "Sozin's Comet, Part 2," *Avatar*.

which we find ourselves. Every last little thing we
do — from eating a meal to taking a walk to playing a
game — has serious implications that ripple in endless
waves: for the Lord misses nothing, just as every falling sparrow has a special place in His infinite heart.[52]
We are never really alone; for He is with us always,
even now. As an aside, we may comment that this
is the grain of truth behind dark totalitarian fantasies of glass houses, through which all of us humans
would allegedly become transparent to each other at
long last.[53] We can see the same perverse dynamic in
how certain elements in our society turn *everything*
about real religion into a caricature, making their
own hideous knock-off versions of what was once
beautiful.[54] Suffice to say that humans are religious
creatures, and that our only real decision is in which
gods we consent to serve.

How does a man go about constructing his own
personality structure, and thereby growing into an
integrated character within the novel of the world?
As is often the case, it may all come down to beauty.
A beautiful personality *is* a moral construction, just
as Jesus was both the most beautiful soul who ever
lived and at the same time the epiphany of final
goodness. In order to achieve such a feat, a man will
need a *key* — a key buried in the heart. Some sages
have spoken of a mysterious power that lives within
the heart chakra: a power that instantaneously tells
a man what is the light and what the dark.[55] It is

---

[52] Matthew 10:29; Dylan, "Every Grain of Sand," *Shot of Love*.
[53] Eggers, *The Circle*.
[54] Lindsay & Nanya, "Postmodern Religion and the Faith of
Social Justice," *Areo*.
[55] Aurobindo, *The Psychic Being*.

an infallible intuition that transcends mere reason, produces a direct and open conduit with none other than the Holy Ghost. Starting with the awakening of that sense within the heart, we can begin to calibrate our own personalities in accordance with our deepest visions of beauty.

A great novel has a central theme; everything about the novel functions as an organic manifestation of that vital core.[56] There is nothing present that contradicts the idea. The other way around, the idea is developed in myriad marvelous ways, while nevertheless remaining *that* idea and nothing else. We have the theme and its variations; we have the core and its emanations. The core is eternal and unchanging, but the emanations exist within ordinary dimensions of space and time, with the flow of a book's pages mimicking the passage of the days. This metaphor is also an image of the nature of God. His heart is one grand Idea, even as it has inexhaustible forms and incarnations. In this context, we may suggest that one thing that makes Jesus special is how He never betrayed the idea that was at the core of what He was. This unfathomable fidelity is part of why He, and no one else, is the Son of God, of one essence with the Author. As we realize that He accepted and fulfilled a burden that would shatter the best of us and leave our minds in tatters, we begin to see His greatness in all its shocking contours.

The moral project, then, has to do with *editing our own personalities,* in much the same way that the poet edits the lines of his stanzas. We must not engage in actions that are dissonant against the core idea,

---

[56] Tolstoy, *Anna Karenina.*

the image of God, that dwells in the depths of each of our hearts. We must cut out such jarring notes if we are to achieve full aesthetic harmony with the deep ideas of our own true personalities. Sin, in this context, is very much about the failure to be a good editor — and the worse the sin, the more grievous the aesthetic error. And starting with discordance in our actions, we may next trace them back to our thoughts and imaginations, with the exact seriousness of Jesus speaking of the adultery committed in the heart.[57] We must seek out every hidden spot and eliminate all recesses within the mind where the darkness could hide; we must aspire to total translucency toward the Light from Above.[58] This praxis is how we begin to abolish the realm of specters and fully pour ourselves out into God's glorious world as the characters He wrote us to become. To shut down the regress into abstracted headspace, once and for all: as a riff on an esoteric poem, we could whimsically give such an endeavor the name of the closing of the Northern Gate.[59]

ENTROPY'S MYSTIQUE

A lot of poets tend to romanticize chaos: the churning of the depths of the soul, which has the power to shake up all the established structures and values of the world. We have, for instance, argued in favor of disorganized religion, on the precise grounds that the institutions that exist today too often ring hollow and false. Such a dynamic reflects

---

[57] Matthew 5:28.
[58] Kierkegaard, *The Sickness unto Death.*
[59] Blake, "Jerusalem," *Complete Writings.*

the legitimate power of chaos: when summoned in the right way, it becomes a force of re-vitalization, incinerating the dead brush that has gathered over time so that new life may burst forth. But chaos also has its shadow side, and we would be foolish to ignore it. A man's life may be enveloped in pure chaos: perhaps he is hooked on drugs; perhaps his finances are in ruins. As he grows more and more desperate, his toxicity will rise to a level where no one could even deal with him any longer, and all his friends will be gone. He may be walking a thin line between a rehab center and a homeless shelter, a county jail and an early grave. Chaos is tailspin; chaos is everything falling apart. Who could envy a man whose life is consumed by chaos?

A delicate dialectic exists between chaos, on the one hand, and *order* on the other.[60] Chaos as such is nothing but entropy and death, just as life is the emergence of increasingly complex order out of nothingness. If chaos is to make a meaningful contribution to life, it needs to be cast into some sort of *form* — for without such a vessel, chaos is like water that lacks an adequate jug for containment: it just spills all over the ground and dries up posthaste, leaving behind nothing but a memory of waste. We can also think about this matter in terms of language and grammar. The English tongue has a structure that we did not create; and if we would like to communicate our ideas to others, then we are obliged to make use of that structure. We can't actually invent our own language — and even if we attempted so bizarre a venture, we would still be relying on the inherent

---

[60] Paglia, *Sexual Personae*; Peterson, *Maps of Meaning*.

structures of grammar within our minds that render language recognizable *as* language, as opposed to mere gibberish.[61] If the poet rejected such basic limits, then there would be nothing left to distinguish him from a yammering schizophrenic.

We could also suggest that there exists a mythical grammar within the human imagination, and that just about all great poets have tapped into those deep structures in some manner. The grammar in question could be understood as a network of archetypes — Shadow and Lady and God, not to mention the entire cast of the Tarot.[62] It is also an epic narrative running from Creation to Apocalypse, passing through the interim of Fall and Redemption.[63] Experience teaches that there *is* such a thing as human nature, and that poetry is the true science of the human soul. What does poetry reveal other than an order that we cannot escape by virtue of our very nature, an order that provides the only meaningful context for our freedom, an order that we must *live through to the end* and not evade or flee?

This is perhaps the point at which we must consider God under His alias of the Heavenly Father. The Holy Ghost has to do with the living spirit of inspired imagination; and Jesus is the Messiah, the supremely creative man. But as we round the Trinity, we encounter the Father: the hidden God, the fountainhead and wellspring of all that is. He is a deity revealed in parts by the prophets and then in full by

---

[61] Chomsky, *On Language.*

[62] Jung, *Aion*; Nichols, *Jung and Tarot*; Unknown Friend, *Meditations on the Tarot.*

[63] Frye, *The Great Code*; Altizer, *The New Apocalypse.*

Jesus; and we may understand Him to represent the
spirit of *objective order* that dwells within the world.
We are talking here about the grammar of language
and imagination, the stability of the cosmic spheres,
the structure of the human flesh. We can celebrate
the subjective imagination all that we want; but at
some point we must admit that there are structures
of mind in here that we did not invent, and that
without them, the whole poetic project would have
been stillborn from the start. We thus arrive at a
framework where the Trinity unites imagination,
order, and human form. Most of us are probably more
comfortable with one or another of these modes; but,
in the end, existential *balance* may require us to hit
a home run with the bases loaded.

An appreciation of chaos should never be outright
dismissed. The watchword here certainly is balance.
There is an ongoing charm in certain kinds of self-
destruction, due to the simple fact that a lot of what
most of us think of as our "selves" stands in need of
serious challenge and renovation: for those selves are
far too opaque and labyrinthine to let in the Light
from Above. In such a scenario, it might become
needful for a man to make like a dissident monk and
set his ego on fire so that something more vital could
have the chance to be reborn.[64] This core truth vali-
dates the ongoing presence of chaos; and the embrace
of chaos is thus not always a matter of succumbing
to nihilism. To reject it altogether would put a man
in the unenviable camp of defending an order merely
because it exists, as if the order was an end in itself.
From our standpoint, then, few things could be more

---

[64] Linklater, *Waking Life*.

despicable than such pharisaism. There will always be something to be said for creative catastrophe.[65] Language has a grammar, but it is true as well that the same grammar that enables the writing of a poem also allows for the declaration of a war. So, what is the nature of the order we embrace, and could there be a better way? Chaos is here to challenge false order, just as irony is here to challenge false values; but chaos alone can't build an enduring life divine, just as what we humans need is not endless irony but a new sincerity.[66] Chaos can be used in favor of the good, but only if we manage to overcome entropy's hypnotic mystique. ❧

---

[65] Nietzsche, "Twilight of the Idols," *A Nietzsche Compendium*.
[66] Wallace, "E Unibus Pluram," *A Supposedly Fun Thing I'll Never Do Again*; Turner, *Metamodernist Manifesto*.

V 🦁 WORLD

POWER'S ABEYANCE

Conservatives tend to dislike an idea that goes by the fancy name of "immanentizing the eschaton."[1] The gist is that left-wing political projects are often geared toward making the Kingdom of Heaven manifest in this world right now — which is generally paired with the belief that capitalized "History" has a direction, and that progressives are on the right side of its arc. The problem with this notion is twofold. First of all, insofar as we humans are fallen, we may or may not have the power to get the Kingdom to show up here without the whole endeavor going very wrong. Second, such a project can easily lead into the utilitarian mindset that it is acceptable to break a few eggs to make an omelet, with the eggs in question being human skulls. If a million human sacrifices would bring an end to History, then the worse among us might find that to be an acceptable tradeoff. And yet, even then, the streets run with blood and the Kingdom never comes — and the scoundrels are always only left with egg on their face.

All decent men and women must certainly oppose that entire revolutionary mindset.[2] Nevertheless, we

---

[1] Voegelin, *The New Science of Politics*.
[2] Camus, *The Rebel*.

are confronted with a gnawing problem, the heart of which is found within the Lord's Prayer: "Your Kingdom come, Your will be done, on Earth as it is in Heaven."[3] These words are inspiring and disconcerting all at once. We may ask: what else could this be other than the Lord's *direct command* to immanentize the eschaton? Jesus very much wanted the Kingdom to become manifest within the dimension of History, and He declares as much in no uncertain terms within His signature invocation. How shall we go about resolving this tension?

First of all, we should take care to avoid a false dichotomy. When conservatives rail against the immanence of the eschaton, their claim is mainly that it is wrong to use politics to try and bring about the Kingdom of Heaven. This point is laudable since politics is the realm of force, whereas the Kingdom is resistant to this sort of coercion and depends entirely on spiritual liberty.[4] Indeed, the use of force in attempts to bring about the descent of Paradise has always been and will remain the fast track to Hell on Earth. But the utter transformation of this world is also an imperative built into the Gospel; therefore, we must suggest that conservatives are mistaken if they imagine that the point of existence is to just endure this life and wait in patience for the next one to come. This world is not some prison where we can only kill time and long for the end. Rather, the name of the game is transfiguration; it is about the fulfillment of the desire expressed in the Lord's Prayer. We thus arrive at the conclusion that the progressives are *correct in*

---

[3] Matthew 6:10.
[4] Berdyaev, *The Destiny of Man.*

their impetus but *wrong in their methods*; whereas conservatives are wrong in their disdain for the impetus, but correct in their skepticism about the methods.

This world is meant to change, but politics is not the vehicle for making that happen. The true method is *poetry* instead. The point has always been the development and growth of the human soul, through which process it no longer even occurs to people to live in such deep ignorance or to treat each other in such brutal ways. Such theosis would have indirect effects on politics, to be sure, but that is far downstream from where we are. Politics in itself can coerce bodies via violence and minds through manipulation, but it is powerless when it comes to catalyzing a true turning of the heart. Since the soul can't be coerced, the genuine transformation of the world also can't be coerced — for such a project begins only with the soul and consists only of the achievement of its freedom as a child of God. We can try to persuade others, but there may be objective limits to the reach of our influence because, again, certain methods are off the table. If people don't wish to listen in freedom, then we cannot make them hear in any other way.

What's left for us is then a long and difficult road. We must absolutely renounce the will to power, the compulsion to impose our desires upon unwilling others. The true project must, instead, consist of a perpetual process of bearing witness. From the standpoint of the soul, this world as such is an unending night: this place is fallen, and the Lord is not sovereign in this dimension. The role of the soular man in this context is *to build a lighthouse and then hold it*. The living heart is the nexus between dimensions, the point at which the Light bleeds in from the other realm.[5] We must aspire to seek and protect that Light, and then to work toward signaling it to all others who may have the eyes to see. We must still remember, however, that this entire process is happening within an overarching nocturnal setting. One soul can light up, and another, and then yet another — producing a luminous lattice of interconnected souls, running through the velvet skies of this world: a candlelight vigil, of sorts. But an individual person can only hold the lighthouse; he can't ring in the Dawn. That prerogative belongs to the Lord alone.

This world is thus a place where the power of the Lord is held in abeyance, and where those dark souls who worship bestial power can often have their way with things. The laws of truth are not the laws of power; and down here in this dimension, truth has no compelling power of its own, save for when it falls upon hearts already open. We cannot ultimately force anyone listen to us, just as we can't reach into the hearts of others and turn those organs around for them. There is thus a certain requisite element of resignation, along with the sense that this world is something of an endurance test. But suppose that the Lord was to make a sudden movement of His own, provoking all hearts in the world in a simultaneous manner. Such an event would be nothing other than *the Second Coming itself* — the universal return of Jesus to this world through the doors of every human heart. In the meanwhile, we are left to our vigil, not knowing when the End will come. It is very much possible that we will not see that victory

---

[5] Del Rey, "Kintsugi," *Did You Know that There's a Tunnel under Ocean Blvd?*

in our mortal lives. But we should just keep our eyes
on the good fight, content in the awareness that come
whatever, it will be worthwhile.[6] The defiance of the
dark is a glorious way for a man to live. And that's
more than enough of a promise.

A STALEMATE FOR THE AGES

A lot of talk exists in our times about the crisis of
liberalism — where "liberalism" here refers not just
to the political left, but rather to the entire modern
project having to do with individual autonomy, sec-
ularism, free enterprise, and related matters.[7] The
main idea is that we have now come to a point where
liberalism can no longer sustain itself; it is tearing apart at the seams, a victim of its own success.
When the autonomy of every single person reaches
its pinnacle, society and culture become consumed by
solipsism due to the absence of a compelling centrip-
etal force, and people are driven to retreat into their
own private realities as the common ground erodes.
This development is often pinned on the collapse of
Christendom (circa the 1960s), which had long pro-
vided Western civilization with a shared metaphysics
and set of values. Therefore, they say, we have since
been left confronted with a brave new world in which
the old tradition is gone and there appears to be
nothing sane to take its place.

We should, however, be quite ambivalent about this
narrative — for we are called to be dyed-in-the-wool
lovers of liberty who find the foreseeable alternatives
unacceptable. A world in which every person has the

---

[6] Camus, *The Myth of Sisyphus.*
[7] Deneen, *Why Liberalism Failed.*

full autonomy to develop his or her own potentials to the fullest: that's the only sort of world that a decent man could desire. To want anything else for all of our fellow images of God is to flirt with fascism and cut deals with the Devil; and there is no use mincing words about the matter.[8] As one intelligent man says: "Human nature is not a machine to be built after a model, and set to do exactly the work prescribed for it, but a tree, which needs to grow and develop itself on all sides, according to the tendency of the inward forces that make it a living thing."[9] This present work itself is one of the fruits of my own tree's unfolding. Knowing how much this process has meant to me, I couldn't imagine denying it to anyone else. We must consider such mutuality to be a non-negotiable condition of any world that we would wish to build.

There is a problem, however. Life seems to demonstrate that most people have trouble living with this sort of liberty, which they experience first and foremost as loneliness, atomization, and the loss of meaning. They are not wrong to feel this way. In a traditional community, the values and narratives are set in stone over the course of many generations, and people can live and die knowing that their grandchildren's world will be the same one they inhabited. By contrast, things move very fast in our world; changes appear to be on a steady path of acceleration, as our globalized society works to dissolve even those bonds that have held out this long.[10]

---

[8] Dostoevsky, *The Brothers Karamazov*; Hart, *Tradition and Apocalypse*.

[9] Mill, *On Liberty*.

[10] Bauman, *Liquid Love*.

Some of us enjoy the freedom of invention; but when it comes to our species as a whole, it may sometimes well seem like a net negative. This thought is not meant to set up a dichotomy between elite overlords and the unwashed masses. To love liberty is to want it for all, or at least to refrain from actively impeding the freedom of others. It is easy to feel nostalgia for shared structures — but on that front, we would do well to think of those who would get branded with scarlet letters.[11] The underlying problem, however, still cannot be shrugged off; for, in the end, it will come for us all. When people feel atomized and desperate, they are liable to take matters into their own hands. History amply demonstrates that totalitarianism always rears its undead head when people feel alone and have nothing left to believe in, failed by the myths of their cultures. That's the point at which they begin to long for a demagogue to save them from themselves.[12] Whether it's nativism and xenophobia on the right or culty intersectionalist garbage on the left, it is quite obvious that people are trying to construct a shared cesspool into which they can plunge their frightened and traumatized selves — a dark parody of baptism.

We humans have a natural longing for community, as well as a need to feel ensconced within a grander whole that transcends our own puny egos. Liberalism, by its own internal logic, has produced a world in which the fulfillment of these needs has become less and less possible for an increasing number of people. Whether due to the depredations of the economy

---

[11] Hawthorne, *The Scarlet Letter.*
[12] Arendt, *The Origins of Totalitarianism.*

or the cultural collapse of shared values, the point remains valid: liberalism promised freedom, but it has produced a material reality in which we have only succeeded in making ourselves miserable.

We see yet another twist. It is perhaps true that liberalism has failed us, but that leaves unanswered the crucial question: *what's the alternative?* Surveying the lay of this land gives us little cause for hope. There are, for example, the people known as integralists, those who want to impose Catholic sharia on the free world.[13] This venture would be outright comical if it weren't such a sad sign of where we are. And then we have the progressives, who, if they had it their way, would make it illegal to utter the ancient notion that our race was created man and woman. Clearly, these are not the best of times. This point calls attention to a basic thesis: namely, that *the alternative to liberalism is theocracy.* If liberalism is understood as a world in which people are free to develop their selves without the threat of coercion or death, then the absence of liberalism must always spell theocracy — a world in which people are forced to adhere to a collective definition of what is real and good.

There is a quote I know that tends to cause some consternation among conservatives: "At the heart of liberty is the right to define one's own concept of existence, of meaning, of the universe, and of the mystery of human life."[14] This gets to the core of the crisis of liberalism. When the guiding principle of a nation is nothing but pure individual autonomy,

---

[13] Ahmari, "The New American Right," *First Things.*
[14] Anthony Kennedy, in Ahmari, "Justice Kennedy's Mystical Jurisprudence," *Commentary.*

it becomes impossible to synthesize a shared culture. But the opposite of defining the mystery of life for ourselves is to have someone else do it for us, and that notion should be enough to turn our stomachs.[15] Liberalism is thus tragic: Icarus-esque, its greatest promise seems to imply its own self-destruction. That leaves us with an unsustainable liberalism, on the one hand, and an unacceptable totalitarianism on the other. This is a stalemate for the ages; and if there is a meaningful way forward (aside from the Rapture), then it seems impossible to discern the contours of that historical path from the present juncture. Only time will tell.

HORIZON OF THE MIND

We are probably too hasty in calling some of our past actions "mistakes", at both the individual and collective levels. The problem is that we tend to evaluate an action, in retrospect, by the criterion of whether it produced the desired outcomes — which is a rather silly way of thinking about the question. Instead, we need to consider what knowledge we had at the time, and whether it would have been possible for us to choose better, knowing what we knew.[16] Maybe an action resulted in good effects or maybe it resulted in bad ones; but either way, the quality of our *decision process* may not have mattered much at all. Some mistakes are obvious as such even as they are happening, and such errors of judgment could be chalked up to straightforward idiocy and cognitive bias. But there also exists an entirely other

---

15 Blake, "Jerusalem," *Complete Writings*.
16 Taleb, *Black Swan*.

class of actions that are not quite mistakes, even if they failed to produce the intended results.

Life is lived forward but remembered in reverse.[17] When we look around our world today, much of what we see is chaos, with the more mad or inspired among us making efforts to discern the relevant patterns in the great soup of it all. But when we look back at what has happened, we act as if everything was self-evident — and we thus forget that the people of the past were also groping in the relative dark, just like us. It is difficult if not impossible to see beyond this horizon of the mind: time curves and turns away from us, toward a place where our vision cannot follow. We can thus affirm that a fundamental absence of perspective is surely responsible for our age's mania for re-litigating the past, condemning historical figures on the basis of current moral standards. We forget that even within the living memory of our own lives, almost everyone held views (such as marriage being the syzygy of woman and man) that today's progressives insist are enough to damn us to the status of pariah. Then they act shocked that some of us still believe in the old ways, as if there was anything remarkable about that; as if the breakneck pace of their own flux weren't the truly odd phenomenon.

A radical contingency is built into history. It is as though we are proceeding in a fog, unable to see more than a few steps ahead, making the best of a bad time — and nothing *has* to happen until it actually does.[18] Then the people of the future will tell absurd

---

[17] Kierkegaard, *Concluding Unscientific Postscript.*
[18] Kundera, *The Curtain*; Tolstoy, *War and Peace.*

stories about how we knew what we were doing, and if we were there to hear them, then we would grimly grin. The problem grows even more ridiculous when we realize that, from the eternal standpoint, *every* era of this world has been pretty rotten. Some things may have been bad even by the standards of their own time; but, then again, is that itself not also true of any and all times? Our reluctance or refusal to receive the Gospel and seek the Kingdom knows no temporal limits. Much the opposite: it certainly looks to be a perennial feature of our fallen human condition; and we must agree that the line between good and evil runs not between social groups, but rather right down the middle of every human heart.[19]

Is there really any such thing as "progress" at all? On the one hand, it is clear that the notion of social or moral progress is a fallacy that has been built upon a false analogy with technology and science. Progress does exist in the latter area: medicine today is lightyears superior to what it used to be, and a small computer in every pocket far surpasses what many of the ancients might have imagined when they spoke of magic. What is also true, however, is that while we no longer look to the ancient Greeks for their medicine, we still seek them for their literature; and the flow of the millennia has done nothing to detract from our appreciation of such works or their ability to speak to us (insofar as we haven't grown too dumb to comprehend them).[20]

The human heart doesn't change in any significant way; its structural parameters have been more or less

---

[19] Solzhenitsyn, *The Gulag Archipelago.*
[20] Aeschylus, *The Oresteia.*

the same from the start. The whig theory of history is probably modeled on the whig theory of life: just as we would all like to imagine that our own lives trace a continual arc of improvement, we want to think that our species is always getting better as well, and that the arc of history thus bends toward the promised land. Wisdom, however, suggests a more cynical (and cyclical) pattern of growth and collapse, rise and decline — which, after all, is what happens to any organism.[21]

Is this all there is, though? Our guts suggest that there must be more; that although history undeniably moves in cycles, it is not a flat circle; that the circle is granted an additional dimension and morphs into a *spiral*.[22] The supersession of the Age of the Father by the Age of the Son — of the Old Testament by the New — seems very much like genuine soular progress at the level of *gestalt*, or what is conceivable for our human race as a whole.[23] There is the entrance and debut of something truly new. The horizon expands, even as people can still remain as awful today as they ever were. Likewise, the imminence of the Age of the Holy Ghost and the Everlasting Gospel suggests that the spiral is not done rising yet. Indeed, we may dare to imagine that after the rise and decline may come *regeneration*, a new life from the grave. We thus shouldn't be too quick to dismiss the notion of "progress" altogether, even as vital progress is not the arithmetic function that some may wish to imagine. If History does progress, then it does so in the

---

[21] Vico, *New Science*; Barzun, *From Dawn to Decadence*.
[22] Pizzolato & Fukunaga, *True Detective, Season 1*.
[23] Joachim of Floris, in Frye, *On Religion*.

dimension of *narrative*, much the same as a Russian novel or a symphony by Beethoven: not linear moral improvement, but a rising of dialectical tensions and an increase in the density of dramatic run-ins; an intensifying recurrence of the original theme; the onset of crises and epiphanies, leading toward the final denouement — first slowly, and then all at once.[24]

THE KING'S BANNER

It cannot help but make us laugh when someone says that the most important thing is to just "be a good person." We could only wish that the matter was as self-evident as that, and that such a statement was anything other than an excellent example of begging the question. The "good" is by no means as obvious as people think it is; and if we persist in thinking otherwise, then that is only because we have been so conditioned by our culture that it doesn't even occur to us to imagine any other possibilities. The fact that people still think it is important to be good is heartening, in any event. The problem is that such a vague and thin definition has no chance of weathering the storms that surely wait ahead. It is like the coyote in the old cartoons: the trick only works so long as no one looks down. Sooner or later, we will be compelled to know that the foundation has been long since gone.

The only truly legitimate form of governance is the monarchy of Heaven, in which the Lord does not compel our obedience by force, but rather only draws us in with love. But given that politics is a

---

[24] Tolstoy, *Anna Karenina*; Beethoven, "Symphony No. 9," *Les 9 Symphonies*.

reality down here in this fallen world, we should probably address it, even if only for a moment. For all the political conflicts of these times, most folk still don't reject certain fundamental values — values such as justice and equality and freedom. Different people interpret those things in very different ways; but whatever they believe, they still tend to defend their beliefs in the name of such values. We should perhaps ask: *why*, after all, does freedom matter to conservatives? And why does equality matter to progressives? And why does justice matter to just about everyone? Such assumptions are very telling.[25]

It is common to speak of the separation of church and state (and we can define "church" here as any system of transcendent values). This separation is by no means natural or inevitable; rather, it is a radical anomaly when considered through any historical lens.[26] Most cultures have assumed as a matter of course that religion should be woven into every single aspect of life — which, truth be told, makes substantial sense. Such an ethos was still active during the Middle Ages in the West, and the Islamic world to this day opposes the idea that the church and state should in any way be separate. Indeed, they would consider such a notion to be blasphemy. The separation is thus unique to a particular culture, and it is not at all a human universal. If we take it for granted, that just means it has been in the air of our own culture for so long that we no longer even think to wonder where it came from or how it emerged.

---

[25] Nietzsche, "On the Genealogy of Morals," *A Nietzsche Compendium.*
[26] Taylor, *A Secular Age.*

The "state" is nothing but a collection of people who are organized in a particular way within a given society. The structure of the state reflects a culture's notions about how people should live among each other — which means that the state *follows* from fundamental beliefs about the nature of reality (which is to say the church). The modern West has long affirmed that all humans are created equal and have inherent rights that can't be taken away by anyone else. But such a proposition is not self-evident at all. Rather, it's a quite particular concept about the nature of man, and it emerged within one culture and not others. Ultimately, the separation of church and state is rooted in the Gospel: it comes from the fact that Jesus wasn't a political revolutionary and that He instructed His followers to render unto Caesar what belonged to him.[27] This command established a basic schism between the realm of politics and the realm of the spirit. The catch is that the value of separating church from state is *itself* the product of one particular "church" — namely, the church that was the foundation of what became Christendom. As much as the historical Church used coercion and violence to bring folk into the fold, it carried a Gospel that testified against such heinous hypocrisy at every single turn. Such a scenario is rather different from, say, Muhammed's straightforward embrace of conversion by the sword.

All values must come from somewhere. If we think that we somehow just "know," then we should at least understand that this is a rather modern view of the matter — a sort of faith in an inner light that tells

27 Matthew 22:21.

man how to live. In our project, we actually do affirm something of this order, albeit with the caveat that the inner light itself only comes from the Logos who made all that is.[28] Justice, freedom, equality, all the rest: these things are, at their core, values that spring from Jesus. If those values are indeed universal, then that is only because the Gospel is meant for every human heart and because Jesus is the hero of the universal religion of the living soul. There is no such thing as "natural religion," as a lucid glance at Nature could tell us well enough.[29] Nature is rather brutal in her fallen state; and within her own domain, power and violence are too often the name of the game. The values that decent humans cherish are literally *supernatural* in their origins, just as all true religion is by definition revealed. If such values seem ordinary today, then we may suggest that's only because He has by now dwelt among us for so long. The defense of such values is always carried out under the King's banner, whether we know it or not.

This perspective also provides another way to consider the crisis of liberalism. The people who first generated liberalism — and in particular, the American experiment, which was the greatest historical epiphany of liberalism — were immersed in a biblical understanding of the world. Reading documents from that era, we are taken aback by the extent to which the leaders unabashedly invoked the name of Providence.[30] Liberalism emerged within Christendom

---

[28] John 1:3.
[29] Paglia, *Sexual Personae*; Blake, "There Is No Natural Religion," *Complete Writings*.
[30] Washington, "Resignation of Military Commission," *National*

and among people who, for the most part, took the values of the faith for granted. Liberalism is only procedural: it is a way for people with different values to live together without killing each other, even as it is incapable of producing values of its own. Now it looks very much like we are running on fumes and out of credit. How long will we continue to reap the benefits of a revelation that we, in our idiot pride, have come to deny?[31] We are being carried by mere momentum, riding on the waves of the patience and the grace — but this cannot go on forever. All things die when cut off from their roots, and our civilization will prove to be no different. The only answer is to return to the beginning, reclaim the genesis of the values we cherish.

THE LAME CRUSADES

Human beings live ensconced within heroic frames of reference, and there is nothing we can do about that, even if we wanted: it is just in our nature.[32] Myth and religion were the traditional ways that people came to terms with their deep need for meaning and communion. In these latter days, a lot of people carry on as if those longings belonged to the adolescence of our species, having now outgrown them. This is radically false, of course. People with that mindset tend to be the most fanatical of us all: they think in religious categories while not even understanding that they are doing so; and such absence of self-knowledge leads to predictable insecurities. They

Archives.
[31] Guardini, *The End of the Modern World.*
[32] Jacobs, "After Technopoly," *The New Atlantis.*

tend to double down and affirm their dogmas with increasing vehemence, only made all the more passionate by their ignorance, as atavistic forces control them from behind their own backs.[33]

Modern progressives very much fit the bill in this regard. Could any doubt remain that the ideology of this camp is really a system of degraded Christian heresies?[34] They take the prophecy of the End Times and turn it sideways, believing that "History" will end in Heaven — located in the *future*, not eternity — right after they have achieved their political project. Small wonder, then, that all differences of opinion become very intense for progressives: for the envisioned conflict is between those who are marching in their deity's united front versus those obstructing the advent of Paradise. With mundane stakes inflated quite that high, little room remains for dialogue or compromise.

We may also observe that for the progressives, the doctrine of climate change fulfills the precise function of apocalypse. Of course, the weather may well be changing, and Nature is surely getting moodier as our world continues to abuse her. When considering the possibility of human extinction, however, our minds might whimsically drift toward the vast expanses of uninhabited land across Canada or Russia or Greenland. If the earth does catch a fever, then presumably much of the ice would melt, and these places would become much more appealing for long-term habitation. Taking advantage of the new scenario

---

[33] Father John Misty, "Pure Comedy," *Pure Comedy*.
[34] Lindsay & Nanya, "Postmodern Religion and the Faith of Social Justice," *Areo*.

would require migration, of course; and the current geopolitical landscape, with its arbitrary invisible lines in the ground, might not survive. But we would do well to raise an eyebrow against anyone who has such little faith in the demonstrable resilience of our species...

The idea here is not to outline the most scientifically plausible scenario, but rather to illustrate the way that the ideological mind takes complex facts and twists them into pat narratives that suit its own purposes. Such things happen because humans are religious creatures, and none of us could ever avoid this destiny in the long run.[35] The adherents of woke ideology are just as religious as anyone else; indeed, we can go so far as to say that they are devout members of their own petty cult. Modern progressivism is a moribund effort to find a meaningful path forward, a toxic heathen heresy for which we cannot spare much but pity and contempt.

What do we fight for? We cannot say "nothing," for human nature cannot accommodate such a response. Our condition compels us to invent or discover some sort of meaning to the flux of the world; and while we may decline to believe in one god or another, there is no such thing as rejecting the gods altogether.[36] We shall all end up believing in some deity — and if it isn't the Lord of life and love, then it will be one of the false gods of power. We may also formulate this celestial fight as the conflict between *fascism* versus *romance*, when those terms are considered expansively as symbols of mindsets.

---

[35] Becker, *The Denial of Death*.
[36] Polikoff, *In the Image of Orpheus*.

The original fascist fallacy consists of loving abstract ideas more than people: real persons, in all their folly and sin and messy freedom. Fascism is always about using power and coercion to control people, change what they are — a parody of the Gospel's promise to make them new. It is the exact opposite with romance, which is about focusing on the actual living person, in all their sadness and wonder and glory. Family and friendship and romantic love are the paths that most folk take to seeing things this way, and such an ethos is ultimately rooted in the vision of the Lord as an individual person, unique and irreplaceable in value.

People embark on lame crusades when they don't have much to live for and when their lives are devoid of the ordinary things that are supposed to lend some meaning. Then they throw their lots in with highfalu-tin abstractions as part of an effort to cast themselves in some faux-heroic light. They miss the reality and grit of the soular call from Above. They remove them-selves from their own actual lives in order to pursue fantasies that have little to do with them — and then they call that "compassion," in order to make them-selves feel justified and good. It is remarkable, is it not, how so many people who care about "humanity" in the abstract have so demonstrably little care for actual living humans?[37] Idea takes precedence over reality; abstraction rules over life. We may acknowledge that the desire to change everything is respectable, for there is so much in the way we all live now that surely must be altered. We could even go so far as to suggest that God must hate America by now, just as He has always hated self-righteous empires; we could well soon add

---

[37] Dostoevsky, *Demons.*

our name to the infernal list of Rome and Babylon and
Egypt. But the progressives have lost all comprehension
of the soular realm and its prerogatives; while on the
other end, most of the conservatives just sputter in
the voice of specters, defending what is already dead.
Who will sing the vital word of the regeneration? That
destiny seems to beckon.

IMMANENT EMANATION

Our endeavor sees religion from the standpoint of
its genesis. At that beginning, no formal structures or
legal codes exist; there is just a man — the prophet —
who has gotten himself consumed by an overwhelming vision.[38] He then goes forth into the world to find
allies and friends, and to share that vision with all
comers. Most folk will of course react with hostility,
for the simple reason that the prophet must sound
like a madman to them, speaking of a reality that
threatens their own. But some feel compelled and
begin to listen. Then the prophet passes on, and his
audience is left making sense of him on their own
terms. *This* is the point at which organized teachings
begin to emerge: it is how others attempt to absorb
and transmit a revelation that would otherwise go
straight over most heads. The point remains, however,
that the heart of the religion is still the prophetic
epiphany. Structures grow up around it like the shell
of a mollusk, but those structures themselves are not
the meaning. Rather, they are a *form* for the original
content, always subject to revision and improvement.
The prophet's vision itself is infallible, but nothing
that comes after could claim that mantle.

---

[38] Jonah 1:17.

Any artist could tell us that form does matter: indeed, one of the obsessions of such a man is to generate the perfect form to make manifest all of his content.[39] At some level, the content doesn't "really" exist without its form, in the same sense that a word does not exist until it is expressed. An incredible magic occurs when a word drifts out from a poet's head and onto the page — the alchemy of the formless taking on its proper garments. But it is still true that content dictates form, and that the validity of form can only be confirmed through an appeal to content. The form of a book is what the underlying vision commands it to be; it has no independent claim to fame all of its own. A shimmering form devoid of worthwhile content: that would be the essence of pharisaism. Such a state of affairs tends to enrage the prophet because, not only does he recognize how much has been lost, he also perceives the hollow shell as a con that has been pulled on people naive enough to mistake it for the real thing, confusing art with artifice.[40]

The insight at hand can be applied to Christendom. First there was Jesus, the seal of the prophets with the earth-shaking vision. He generated a community and a way of life that were the proper form for the content He had brought down from Heaven; and He went through existence as a *living poem*, the perfect manifestation of content into form, the Word into flesh.[41] But then He left this realm, and people who had not quite seen what He had were charged with propagating what they had known of the Truth.

---

[39] Rank, *Art and Artist*; Howard, *Chance or the Dance?*.
[40] Matthew 23:27.
[41] John 1:1.

Eventually, a man named Constantine turned it into the religion of empire — and we may say that it all went downhill from there. The clergy gained power, and then they were compelled to do all the things that people do to keep it, including, but not limited to, allying with the princes of this world.[42] They persecuted their own, took up the sword. The material form of the Church of Peter grew extravagant in the process; but what of the content of the founding revelation, the Truth of the living soul?

That is a rhetorical question, of course. The radical edge of Magdalene's original vision has been all but lost in history's shuffle; for such content would be rather useless when it comes to producing a form of material power. We have forgotten that Easter should make rebels of us all.[43] Jesus was a vagabond who never stopped pointing out the antithesis between the logic of the Kingdom and that of this world. Who among us could imagine, then, that He wanted the HQ of His Church to be a sovereign state, or a network of principalities, or indeed anything having to do with the structures of this fallen realm? Then we must begin to think of what might be a better form. Perhaps art gives the best of all hints; for true art is always a window into the Kingdom (either in a direct manner or via converse images of Hell). Art is the unity of content and form: the best example there is for now, short of the Gospel, of a word that wishes to be spoken, expressed in the precise manner in which it wants to be said. The achievement of this unity — but in the medium of *life* and not just the

---

[42] MacCulloch, *Christianity: The First Three Thousand Years.*
[43] Hart, *The Doors of the Sea.*

created object — is our mission.[44] The goal is theosis, through which the image of God within us finds its perfect expression via the medium of the particular creatures that we are.

We could restate the old doctrine of salvation by both faith and works as a matter of the unity of content of form, as well as a unity of identity and performance.[45] So long as the way a man lives is contrary to what his poetic vision mandates, a breach exists between identity on the one hand and performance on the other; and the incarnation would be cursed to remain incomplete. The word "performance" in this regard has nothing to do with a sense of fakeness or facade. Rather, it is just a reflection of the fundamental fact that in this realm we live in, the human soul is not perceptible to others in a direct manner — and we are all obliged to invoke *personas*, or masks, in order to get our point across the perilous bridge between the outside and the within.[46] Life requires us to perform many acrobatic translations. Form out of content is the way that any art works; and it is also how soular vision is turned into an adequate mode of existence. Perhaps the future of the historical world will pan out in the same way as well. If the current world is ugly, then that's because it is, on the aggregate, a mirror of ourselves. In order to really transform the world, then, what's needed is nothing less than a universal mutation in the heart of Adam Kadmon, enacted by a movement of the Holy Ghost.

---

[44] Berdyaev, *The Meaning of the Creative Act.*
[45] James 2:17.
[46] Hashino, *Persona 5.*

ON PROVERBS AND PROPHETS

When we are young (or maybe in an altered state of consciousness), we are wont to believe that the spirit can conquer everything, that the walls of this world are made of nothing more than paper tissue to be rearranged via pure fiat of subjective poetic will.[47] But as we get older, we get a little more tired; we realize that for all our imaginings, the world is more solid than we thought. We find that its barriers are made not of confetti, but of concrete — and that rage against them as we might, they still tend to confine much of what could happen in our lives. It is also unhelpful that most people's minds appear to be more or less invested in the societal status quo. When a burgeoning poet is young, he may imagine that everyone will be just thrilled to hear of the visions of beauty that he wants to share with them. It is only later that a sad fact occurs to him: namely, that the usual reaction of the mass man to new beauty is to want to throttle it, so that he can get back to his somnambulism in peace and quiet.[48]

It is almost surprising how little Jesus has to say about most of the things that make up everyday human life. Finances and family come to mind: a man who takes Jesus at His word could probably never have a stable home or commit to the responsible rearing of children — things that are priorities for the vast majority of people. To have children is to worry about whether they will be able to get a good education, which is the sort of worldly concern that seems to be in tension with a soular call. We thus shouldn't be

---

47 Vaneigem, *The Revolution of Everyday Life.*
48 Girard, *I See Satan Fall like Lightning.*

surprised that many who have felt such a destiny have tended to be awful family men, if they even bothered with that endeavor at all.[49] The New Testament gets at the *depth* of human life, but not its *breadth*; there are all kinds of things not even touched on by that text. The Gospel does indeed reveal the deepest meaning of this existence, but it gives few clues about how to live on the ground like a normal mammal.

The call of the prophet is a phenomenon that happens, and a man subjected to it may well end up sacrificing the breadth for the depth, in the event that this proves to be required of him. One prophet puts the matter with a degree of poignancy that leaves no room for doubting the reality of the experience: "But if we're afraid to do the dictates of our angels, and tremble at the tasks set before us; if we refuse to do spiritual acts because of natural fears and desires — who can describe the dismal torments of such a state! I too remember the threats that I heard! If you, who are organized by Providence for communion, refuse, and bury your talent in the earth: then even though you'll have natural bread, sorrow and desperation will pursue you through life — and after death, shame and confusion in the face of eternity."[50] Such a man certainly cannot betray his call. We are still left with the fact that such proclamations provide a very *thin* conception of what life is; and in fact, this point brings our attention to the true value of the Old Testament: the compendium that makes a valiant attempt to address the breadth of life.

---

[49] Polikoff, *In the Image of Orpheus*; Garff, *Søren Kierkegaard: A Biography*.
[50] Blake, *Complete Writings*.

Different things in the Old Testament seem to be true in different ways. We have, of course, the prophets, who prefigure the Heavenly Father of Jesus and go a good way toward the ultimate depth of existence. Then there are also other sections, such as the Book of Proverbs, that seem to more or less contradict such a radical vision. Overall, the proverbs tend to counsel prudence — whereas it would be difficult to think of anything *less* prudent than the inspired ravings of the prophets.[51] The proverbs are about worldly, natural wisdom, whereas the prophets are about supernatural revealed vision. Must these two angles be locked in an eternal antagonism with each other; or is there some sort of treaty they could sign in order to reach a higher integration that respects the truths contained on each of their venerable sides?[52]

The question at hand fundamentally has to do with how a man is supposed to live in the world. In his adolescence, it is easy for a man to believe that his own passion will just consume everything; that there wouldn't even be much of a world left, much less the question of how to live within it. But then he may turn 30-years-old or so; and, much to his wonder and chagrin, he may discover that the world still exists. Then a long road ahead begins to show itself, and the inevitable question rears its head: *how to live?* How to develop a mode of existence that is both fulfilling in the short run and sustainable in the long? Jesus didn't have to worry about this question, dying as He did in full youthful splendor. We thus circle back to the fact that even the Gospel

---

51 Proverbs 8:12; Heschel, *The Prophets.*
52 Cohen, "Treaty," *You Want It Darker.*

doesn't address the breadth of human life. The legend of Jesus says it all about the depth of excruciating pain and love in the blaze of one glorious weekend; but it doesn't address the everyday wear and tear, the process of age and decay or related challenges. When it comes to such matters, we may well find that the proverbs have better suggestions to offer than the prophets.

A deep danger dwells in attempting this sort of synthesis of the depth and the breadth, which has to do with the fact that no one really likes listening to the prophets. It would be easy for what began as a balanced perspective to degenerate into crass blindness, with the depth of life getting more or less dismissed because of its tendency to trouble the placid breadth. Another way to say the same thing is that even though the proverbs give good counsel, a man who believed in nothing but the proverbs would risk becoming some bourgeois philistine, lukewarm as dishwater.[53] Poets may have a sort of constitutional immunity against this error — but they then suffer from the converse problem, wont as they are to deny prudence and cast themselves into the fire. There is no easy answer to this dilemma; rather, it is a paradox that must be worked out through the cultivation of living wisdom. An intellectual answer delivered in the abstract would just muddy the waters further, reducing a complexity that insists on its own integrity. We should just at least keep the goal in focus, and then reckon as we must.

---

[53] Revelation 3:16.

THE RIDDLE OF THE REALMS

Resentment must be the most toxic feeling in the world. A man begins to feel it when he thinks that he *deserves* something, but that the world has failed to give him his proper due. The precursor of resentment is thus always a sense of entitlement. A man who gets caught up in this sort of thought loop becomes repulsive and self-absorbed to a greater and greater extent, and, taken to its terminus, the process could only end in self-enclosed, narcissistic madness.[54] Such a man looks around the world and only thinks about what has been denied to him. The very sight of the happiness of others becomes enough to contort his face along the arc between misery and rage. It is rather similar to how a man in love feels joy at the sight of other couples; whereas a man who is heartbroken may be inclined to take every such vision as a personal insult. In short, we are quite susceptible to turning inputs from the world into mirrors of our own souls.

Resentment tends to give rise to a false scale of values, through which the "losers" — burning up inside as they are — seek to establish a world in which they and their kind are the ones who reign supreme and the others will be made to suffer what they have felt.[55] Cut off from a world that cares nothing for them, they turn to demented fantasies of revenge instead.[56] The worst of it is that the poet, marginal in his own world as he probably is, may almost relate to such figures: for is there really any bright man

---

[54] Kierkegaard, *The Concept of Anxiety.*
[55] Nietzsche, "On the Genealogy of Morals," *A Nietzsche Compendium.*
[56] Phillips, *Joker.*

today who could in all honesty say that he has never felt resentment sink its fangs into his own heart? But this point is where the intervention of the Gospel changes everything. As the Lord said: "If they hate you, know that they hated Me first."[57] These words require a basic re-interpretation of the very nature and meaning of this world we all live in. It suggests that a radical mystery is built into the fabric of things, and that any notions of what we "deserve" must take a back seat in the face of this gargantuan enigma.

To believe that we deserve things is to assume that we know how this world is supposed to work, and that a linear connection is supposed to prevail between goodness on the one hand and "success" on the other. But that is an unjustified premise (even if we grant that we are "good" in the first place, which is itself a massive ask). There is absolutely nothing about the world that points to this sort of crude justice being a serious organizing principle of our cosmos. Rather, if there is any justice, then it is quite often indirect and poetic, available only to the eyes that are able to see it. No answers can be found when gazing with the clay eyes of this world.

A man could live in a mansion, and the world may say of him that he has done very well; but he may have neither family nor friends to speak of, and his internal life could be a vision of Hell itself. The soular judgment thus emerges that this man has failed at life, and that what appears to be his mansion is in fact the mausoleum of a living death, far worse than the literal thing. But the rich man may still remain rich; poverty of soul need not change a thing about

[57] John 15:18.

that. This is the sort of mystery addressed by Jesus in His most outlandish moments. We see it in His declaration that the first shall be last and the last shall be first, presented as a coda to a parable about how a man who shows up to work at the end of the day gets the same pay as a man who's been there from the start.[58] Such sayings could only be intended as a direct offense against our commonsensical notions of entitlement and just deserts. Jesus suggests a paradox and a generosity that wreak havoc on whatever we think we mean by our self-righteous appeals to "justice," while at the same time pointing to the hidden structure of the soular realm.

Some may accuse Jesus of being the paragon of resentment, speaking as He did of a whole new reality marked by reversed values.[59] But the mad gambit of the Gospel is in fact to *repent* of resentment: for the Gospel is about communion, and there is nothing that harms this cause more than that dark venom. We already have our reward, and to expect the world's rewards as well amounts to a simple misunderstanding of what is going on. Success would be nice, of course; but that is just not in the nature of the game — and living in the midst of this world of false values, the soular man must accept the irony of his own fate.[60] The other realm's reward is there for the taking, and it is first and foremost the distraction of resentment that can get in the way of a man accessing it — in which case he will have the reward of neither this world nor the other.

[58] Matthew 20:1-16.
[59] Nietzsche, "The Antichrist," *The Nietzsche Compendium.*
[60] Bantock, *The Morning Star.*

Even that is not quite it, though. It is better to consider the world not as a logical system, but rather as a grand riddle, with every scenario a man encounters in his life being one of its myriad manifestations. We should adopt the standpoint of perennial student, always looking with new eyes and beginner's mind at the life that is in front of us.[61] Whatever we know, it could never be enough to justify passing a summary judgment on the world; for that would be nothing less than a usurpation of the Lord's own prerogative. Our fundamental question must be: how to make the world come alive again? The point is to ring the grand bell at the bottom of everything, and to thereby send benevolent shockwaves across the entire collective imagination. We can identify toxic patterns of thought and feeling by the litmus test of whether they make the world brighter or do nothing but dim it. When it comes to this riddle, our petty notions of justice are worth so very little. But the Lord isn't like the Sphinx: for He wants us to win; and the correct answer to the riddle doesn't banish Him, but only perpetuates His ongoing incarnation.[62] So, let us not shut down all the magic in a misguided attempt at self-defense, but instead look at the world with open hearts and ponder, in wonder, what its riddle wants to tell us.

PARADIGM OF GOODBYE

We all have a need for community; and in these latter days, most of us suffer from a lack of it. The

---

[61] Merton, *Zen and the Birds of Appetite*; Camus, *Resistance, Rebellion, and Death*.
[62] Sophocles, *Oedipus the King*.

world can be a cold and lonesome place, and the only warmth within this dimension comes from the lives that we share with each other, the solidarity that we build together.[63] So many of us are more atomized than ever, drowned in a social and economic system that cares nothing for human bonds and dissolves all connections faster than we can create them.[64] What's left is a radical alienation that leaves folk coping in the most desperate ways. It surely cannot be a coincidence that people are trying to seek salvation via identity politics at the exact cultural moment when there is no longer real human communion to be had. When will they see that the proliferation of their so-called "identities" reveals nothing so much as the disintegration of the self?

Yet, for all the longings that we have for community, how many of us are actually fit for one, if push comes to shove? To be a part of an old-school community is to limit ourselves by the expectations of others, accept a shared definition of reality, give up the project of self-actualization to the extent that it doesn't comport with whatever's meant by the greater good. We are right to chafe at the prospect of such requirements. If this is what is needed in order to have a community, then, for all the pain of it, maybe we would be better off free and alone — and if liberalism is a problem, then we may have to be a part of it: for many of us have little more than disdain for unchosen bonds. Without such bonds, a community may not have the grit or density or depth to hold together, since anyone could just come and go at will.

---

[63] Camus, *The Rebel.*
[64] Bauman, *Liquid Love*; Houellebecq, *The Elementary Particles.*

There is a deeper conundrum as well. We must know that this world as such is not our home, let alone any little parcel of land upon it. Man is a way-farer, with a soul that comes from Above and shall return there one day.[65] Everything we experience down here in this dimension is transient as a matter of course. Knowing this, how seriously could we take the communities that we form? At best, we are roving caravan bands, keeping each other warm and carrying on with the collective journey; coming together and breaking apart with the movements of the wind; each of us pursuing our salvation; all together, but also alone. A traditional community in a small town, where everyone thinks the same and where they all know our names, which suggests a mixture of both comfort and menace. That sounds like a nice baseline, perhaps, but is it what we really want in the end? Would they not always persecute the outsider, the heretic, the deviant from groupthink?[66]

An anecdote: I was once in the process of leaving a good city. I had been in the doldrums for a while, feeling apathetic about all the things I saw. Then, as soon as I decided that it was time to go, the environ-ment began to light up again. But what I was seeing was what had been there all along: my eyes had just grown dull and jaded across the ordinary grind of the days. In contrast, when I decided to leave, I was within the paradigm of goodbye — and that mindset revealed how valuable everything really was. But why did I need the jolt of a journey to make me see things under the auspices of this radiance? We humans

---

[65] Percy, *Lost in the Cosmos.*
[66] Hawthorne, *The Scarlet Letter.*

are always saying goodbye to this world in general. Time as such is a mystery; within the span of a mere several decades, all of us will be bidding farewell to everything that exists down in this realm. We are wont to ignore this awareness, terrified as most of us are by the prospect of our own mortal end; but by ignoring it, do we not also shut out much of the beauty that shines through this realm, all for a few crumbs of numbed comfort? We have sold off far more than Jacob's brother, while also having lost the sense for why that matters.[67]

To see a part of this world, and then to not see it again — maybe not for a while, maybe not forever: perhaps this teaches us the hard lesson of transience, along with the proper way to appreciate things. We learn that nothing belongs to us; that everything is a gift from Above; that we are here to walk a vagrant's road, and not to hunker down within our own spectral citadels out of a demented illusion of permanence. As the poet says:

> He who binds himself to a joy
> Does the wingéd life destroy
> He who kisses the joy as it flies
> Lives in eternity's sunrise[68]

The horizon of this life is the final goodbye; all of us inhabit carnal forms that are destined to degrade, from gestalt to ash. We may suggest that the new community is forged on the road, via the encounters of kindred souls that have inherent projects held in common; that it is built by the people who have no

---

[67] Genesis 25:33.
[68] Blake, "Eternity," *Complete Writings*.

choice but to be friends, for they just understand each other too well and find themselves upon the selfsame path. It is a unity of freedom and necessity — the development of the soul in accordance with the call that each of us feels from Above, which along the way leads to a convergence of those who have been guided by a single Voice.[69] That, perhaps, is the sort of community that will prevail in the world that comes next.

THE BURNING BUSH

The Burning Bush is the holy ground where the full-fledged tradition of prophecy began, with the Lord's momentous request to Moses that he take off his sandals.[70] Can any poet really resist the impulse to invoke the Burning Bush and kneel before it, any more than he can fail to call down the Pentecostal fire to inspire his mind?[71] The Burning Bush marks the debut of God the liberator, the deity who wants to rescue us humans from Egypt. We are always in captivity within a soular Egypt — and the Lord is indeed here to enact a jailbreak, lead us to the New Jerusalem.

Prophecy has always been a matter of establishing a direct channel with the deity, hearing His voice, conveying the resultant vision. The calling of the prophet has also changed a lot over the course of the ages. The prophets of the Old Testament, for example, come across as rather dour men.[72] They

---

[69] Paz, *The Double Flame.*

[70] Cohen, *The Flame;* Exodus 3:5; Chapman et al., *The Prince of Egypt.*

[71] O'Siadhail, *The Five Quintets;* Esolen, *The Hundredfold: Songs for the Lord.*

[72] Father John Misty, "Pure Comedy," *Pure Comedy.*

also seem to have experienced partial suspensions of their personalities, adopting the voice of the deity Himself in a very direct manner. There was a lot of storm and stress and disturbing imagery, particularly with respect to violence and revenge. Then, with the coming of Jesus, things turned around and the old-fashioned prophets shifted gear, became mystics and saints. Now we have good reason to believe that the dominion of the Everlasting Gospel will be marked by neither the estrangement of the Old Testament era nor the expectancy of New Testament reign, but by a fuller consummation of what was once promised.

If the first age resembles a lovers' quarrel and the second suggests an engagement, then we would have to see the third as a marriage — and the wedding feast is the exact image with which the Book of Revelation closes out the biblical saga.[73] This era should herald a gentler time than we have known: a time in which soular success is already won and made manifest within an eternal present, and in which the manic depression of bygone ages could finally call it a day. An original vision is needed for the way forward from the times we live in. Prophecies in the Age of the Ghost probably sound a little like these magnificent words:

> Expect the end of the world. Laugh.
> Laughter is immeasurable. Be joyful
> though you have considered all the facts.
> So long as women do not go cheap
> for power, please women more than men.

The poem continues:

---

[73] Revelation 19:9.

Go with your love to the fields.
Lie easy in the shade. Rest your head
in her lap. Swear allegiance
to what is nighest in your thoughts.
As soon as the generals and politicos
can predict the motions of your mind,
lose it. Leave it as a sign
to mark the false trail, the way
you didn't go. Be like the fox
who makes more tracks than necessary,
some in the wrong direction.
Practice resurrection.[74]

Yes — we must know that the voice of our Lord does indeed carry this sort of cadence.

The world being what it is, we will always face the temptation to fall back into a lower mode of consciousness. The archons have a deep interest in drawing us into the fallen fold; for, when we dwell upon the frequency of the Ghost, we become untouchable and they can no longer engage in their vampiric absorption of our blood. There is a war going on between the fascists and the romantics of this world. We also know that the Devil desires to keep man and woman apart, knowing full well that their communion would be his death knell. In order to live well, we must adopt a perpetual posture of resistance, engage in a praxis of immunity against the virus that infects all of what folk so naively call reality. We must stay close to the ground, so as to evade the notice of the dark angels.[75]

---

[74] Berry, "Manifesto: The Mad Farmer Liberation Front," *A Country of Marriage*.
[75] Bantock, *The Morning Star*.

Help is always available, if we only dare call upon the holy Name. In these times, however, we have grown apathetic to all forces demonic and divine, preferring instead to confine ourselves to a world as flat as the virtual realms we increasingly inhabit. We have failed to heed the old warning that the Devil's greatest trick is to convince us that he doesn't exist.[76] The net result is that even as a glimmering escape route from the damnation of this place beckons right in front of us, we don't dare to trust our own eyes. Evidently, we would rather just fiddle with the furniture and tell ourselves it isn't all such a bad time, even as we go about the work of building Hell right here and now.

How long did we figure the lie could last? Look around the world today: it very much seems that things are coming apart at the seams. A new life burgeons, wanting to be born — but in the meanwhile, there is the inevitable threat of catastrophe as old orders dissolve and what's next has not yet become manifest. A lot is left up to us, to those among us who are brave enough to take up the mantle. This manifesto is an incitement to become that sort of person and to advance the perennial works of the living soul. The spirit of prophecy lives on, and we are called to bear that fire. This work has perhaps been about a cult — but it isn't at all the brainwashing sort. Folk would be well-advised, however, to go ahead and wash their own brains; for they are probably dirty, having hung out in the mud of the fallen world time out of mind. The traditional baptism is all well and good as

---

[76] Baudelaire, "The Generous Gambler," *Paris Spleen*.

far as this dimension goes, but we must remember what Jesus said to Nicodemus in the depths of night and seek the great sacrament: the baptism by the water and the Holy Ghost, for the true and higher rebirth of the soul.[77] Such is our quixotic project, and that invitation always stands open. ❦

FIN

---

[77] John 3:5; Unknown Friend, *Meditations on the Tarot.*

BIBLIOGRAPHY

Abbott, Edwin. *Flatland: A Romance of Many Dimensions.* Warbler Classics, 2019.

Aeschylus. *The Oresteia.* Trans. Robert Fagles. Penguin, 1984.

Ahmari, Sohrab. "The New American Right." *First Things.* 2019. Available online.

—. "Justice Kennedy's Mystical Jurisprudence." *Commentary.* 2018. Available online.

Alexander, Scott. "Sort by Controversial." *Slate Star Codex.* 2018. Available online.

Altizer, Thomas J.J. *The New Apocalypse: The Radical Christian Vision of William Blake.* Davies Group Publishers, 2003.

Arendt, Hannah. *The Origins of Totalitarianism.* Harcourt Brace Jovanovich, 1973.

Aurobindo, Sri. *The Mother.* Lotus Press, 1990.

—. *The Psychic Being.* Lotus Press, 1990.

Bantock, Nick. *The Morning Star.* Chronicle Books, 2003.

Barnstone, Willis, and Marvin Meyer, editors. *The Gnostic Bible.* Shambhala, 2009.

Barzun, Jacques. *From Dawn to Decadence.* Harper Perennial, 2001.

Baudelaire, Charles. *The Flowers of Evil.* Trans. William Aggeler. Academy Library Guild, 1954.

—. *Paris Spleen.* Trans. Louise Varese. New Directions, 1970.

Bauman, Zygmunt. *Liquid Love.* Polity, 2003.

—. *Liquid Modernity.* Polity, 2000.

Becker, Ernest. *The Denial of Death.* Free Press, 1997.

Beethoven, Ludwig van. *Les 9 Symphonies.* Conducted by André Cluytens. EMI, 2006.

Berdyaev, Nicolas. *The Destiny of Man.* Trans. Natalie Duddington. Semantron Press, 2009.

—. *Dostoevsky: An Interpretation.* Trans. Donald Attwater. Semantron Press, 2009.

—. *The Meaning of the Creative Act.* Trans. Donald A. Lowrie. Semantron Press, 2009.

Berry, Wendell. *A Country of Marriage*. Counterpoint, 2013.

Blake, William. *Complete Writings*. Ed. Geoffrey Keynes. Oxford University Press, 1966.

—. *The Marriage of Heaven and Hell*. Oxford University Press, 1975.

Bob-Waksberg, Raphael. *BoJack Horseman*. Netflix, 2020.

Bon Iver. *22, A Million*. April Base, 2016.

Bridges, James. *Urban Cowboy*. Paramount Pictures, 1980.

Brown, Norman O. *Love's Body*. University of California Press, 1966.

Buber, Martin. *I and Thou*. Trans. Walter Kaufmann. Touchstone, 1971.

Bukowski, Charles. *Betting on the Muse*. Ecco, 2002.

Bulgakov, Mikhail. *The Master and Margarita*. Trans. Richard Pevear and Larissa Volokhonsky. Penguin, 2001.

Burton, Tim. *Dumbo*. Walt Disney Studios, 2019.

Cameron, James. *Titanic*. Paramount Pictures, 1997.

Camus, Albert. *The Myth of Sisyphus*. Trans. Justin O'Brien. Vintage, 1991.

—. *The Rebel*. Trans. Anthony Bower. Vintage, 1992.

—. *Resistance, Rebellion, and Death*. Vintage, 1995.

Carroll, Lewis. *Alice's Adventures in Wonderland*. Bantam Classics, 1984.

Chapman, Brenda, Steve Hickner, and Simon Wells. *The Prince of Egypt*. DreamWorks Pictures, 1998.

Chensvold, Christian. "Rise of the Warrior Monk." *National Review*. 2019. Available online.

Chesterton, G.K. *Collected Works, Volume III*. Ignatius Press, 1990.

Chomsky, Noam. *On Language*. New Press, 1998.

Clements, Ron, and John Musker. *Hercules*. Walt Disney Studios, 1997.

Coen Brothers. *The Big Lebowski*. Gramercy Pictures, 1998.

Cohen, Leonard. *Book of Longing*. Ecco, 2007.

—. *The Flame*. Farrar, Straus and Giroux, 2018.

—. *The Future*. Columbia, 1992.

—. *Various Positions*. Columbia, 1984.

—. *You Want It Darker.* Columbia, 2016.

Del Rey, Lana. *Did You Know that There's a Tunnel under Ocean Blvd?* Interscope, 2023.

—. *Honeymoon.* Interscope, 2015.

Deleuze, Gilles. *Pure Immanence: Essays on a Life.* Trans. Anne Bayman. Zone Books, 2005.

— and Felix Guattari. *A Thousand Plateaus: Capitalism and Schizophrenia.* Trans. Brian Massumi. University of Minnesota Press, 1987.

Deneen, Patrick. *Why Liberalism Failed.* Yale University Press, 2019.

Dobkin, David. *Wedding Crashers.* New Line Cinema, 2005.

Dostoevsky, Fyodor. *The Brothers Karamazov.* Trans. Richard Pevear and Larissa Volokhonsky. Farrar, Straus and Giroux, 2002.

—. *Crime and Punishment.* Trans. Richard Pevear and Larissa Volokhonsky. Vintage, 1993.

—. *Demons.* Trans. Richard Pevear and Larissa Volokhonsky. Vintage, 1995.

—. *The Idiot.* Trans. Richard Pevear and Larissa Volokhonsky. Vintage, 2003.

—. *Notes from Underground.* Trans. Richard Pevear and Larissa Volokhonsky. Vintage, 1994.

Dreher, Rod. "The Gift of Kintsugi Christianity." *The American Conservative.* 2018. Available online.

Dylan, Bob. *Chronicles.* Simon & Schuster, 2005.

—. *Planet Waves.* Asylum, 1974.

—. *Highway 61 Revisited.* Columbia, 1965.

—. *Shot of Love.* Columbia, 1981.

—. *Slow Train Coming.* Columbia, 1979.

Eggers, Dave. *The Circle.* Vintage, 2014.

Eliade, Mircea. *The Sacred and the Profane.* Trans. Willard R. Trask. Harcourt Brace Jovanovich, 1987.

Emerson, Ralph Waldo. *Essays & Lectures.* The Library of America, 1983.

Esolen, Anthony. *The Hundredfold: Songs for the Lord.* Ignatius Press, 2019.

Fallon, Brian. *Sleepwalkers*. Island, 2018.

Father John Misty. *Pure Comedy*. Sub Pop, 2017.

Fehrenbach, TR. *Lone Star: A History of Texas and the Texans*. Da Capo, 2000.

Fincher, David. *Fight Club*. Adapted from Chuck Palahniuk. 20th Century Fox, 1999.

Fitzgerald, F. Scott. *The Great Gatsby*. Scribner, 2004.

Flowers, Brandon. *Flamingo*. Island, 2010.

Fortune, Dion. *The Mystical Qabalah*. Weiser Books, 2022.

Freud, Sigmund. *The Freud Reader*. Ed. Peter Gay. W.W. Norton & Company, 1995.

Fromm, Erich. *Escape from Freedom*. Holt, 1994.

Frye, Northrop. *Fearful Symmetry: A Study of William Blake*. Princeton University Press, 1969.

—. *The Great Code: The Bible and Literature*. Mariner Books, 2002.

—. *On Religion*. University of Toronto Press, 2000.

Garff, Joakim. *Søren Kierkegaard: A Biography*. Trans. Bruce H. Kirmmse. Princeton University Press, 2007.

Gebser, Jean. *The Ever-Present Origin*. Ohio University Press, 1986.

Girard, Rene. *I See Satan Fall Like Lightning*. Trans. James G. Williams. Orbis Books, 2001.

Goethe, Johann Wolfgang von. *Faust*. Trans. Walter W. Arndt. W.W. Norton & Company, 1998.

Gramsci, Antonio. *Prison Notebooks*. International Publishers, 1989.

Greenaway, Gavin. "Through Heaven's Eyes." *Prince of Egypt*. DreamWorks Records, 1998.

Guardini, Romano. *The End of the Modern World*. Intercollegiate Studies Institute, 2001.

Hadot, Pierre. *The Inner Citadel*. Trans. Michael Chase. Harvard University Press, 2001.

Hart, David Bentley. *That All Shall Be Saved: Heaven, Hell, and Universal Salvation*. Yale University Press, 2019.

—. *The Doors of the Sea: Where Was God in the Tsunami?* Eerdmans, 2011.

— . *Tradition and Apocalypse: An Essay on the Future of Christian Belief.* Baker Academic, 2022.

Hashino, Katsura. *Persona 5.* Altus, 2017.

Haskins, Susan. *Mary Magdalen: Myth and Metaphor.* Riverhead Trade, 1995.

Hawthorne, Nathaniel. *The Scarlet Letter.* Canon Press, 2019.

Heschel, Abraham J. *The Prophets.* Harper Perennial, 2001.

Hesse, Hermann. *My Belief: Essays on Life and Art.* Farrar, Straus and Giroux, 1974.

Holy Bible. New King James Version. Thomas Nelson, 2018.

Homer. *The Odyssey.* Trans. Emily Wilson. W.W. Norton & Company, 2017.

Horton, Peter. "Autofac." *Electric Dreams.* Sony Pictures Television, 2017.

Houellebecq, Michel. *The Elementary Particles.* Trans. Frank Wynne. Vintage, 2001.

— . *The Possibility of an Island.* Trans. Gavin Boyd. Vintage, 2007.

Howard, Ron. *A Beautiful Mind.* Universal Pictures, 2001.

Howard, Thomas. *Chance or the Dance?* Ignatius Press, 2018.

Huxley, Aldous. *Brave New World.* Harper Perennial, 2006.

— . *The Perennial Philosophy.* Harper Perennial, 2009.

Jacobs, Alan. "After Technopoly." *The New Atlantis.* 2019. Available online.

Jameson, Fredric. *Postmodernism, or, The Cultural Logic of Late Capitalism.* Duke University Press, 1992.

John of the Cross. *The Collected Works.* Trans. Kieran Kavanaugh and Ottilio Rodriguez. ICS Publications, 1991.

Jung, C.G. *Aion: Researches into the Phenomenology of the Self.* Princeton University Press, 1979.

Jung, Emma, and Marie-Louis von Franz. *The Grail Legend.* Princeton University Press, 1998.

Jusino, Ramon K. *Mary Magdalene: Author of the Fourth Gospel?* 1998. Available online.

Keiper, Caitrin. "Do Elephants Have Souls?" *The New Atlantis.* 2013. Available online.

Kierkegaard, Søren. *The Concept of Anxiety.* Trans. Reidar Thomte. Princeton University Press, 1981.

—. *Concluding Unscientific Postscript.* Trans. Howard V. Hong and Edna H. Hong. Princeton University Press, 1992.

—. *Either/Or, Part I.* Trans. Howard V. Hong and Edna H. Hong. Princeton University Press, 1987.

— *Philosophical Fragments.* Trans. Howard V. Hong and Edna H. Hong. Princeton University Press, 1985.

—. *The Sickness unto Death.* Trans. Howard V. Hong and Edna H. Hong. Princeton University Press, 1983.

Kingsnorth, Paul. "The Basilisk." *Emergence Magazine.* 2020. Available online.

Kirk, Russell. "Ten Conservative Principles." The Russell Kirk Center. 2019. Available online.

Konietzko, Bryan, and Michael Dante DiMartino. *Avatar: The Last Airbender.* Nickelodeon Animation Studio, 2008.

Kundera, Milan. *The Curtain.* Trans. Linda Asher. Harper Perennial, 2007.

—. *The Festival of Insignificance.* Trans. Linda Asher. Harper Perennial, 2016.

—. *Life Is Elsewhere.* Trans. Aaron Asher. Harper Perennial, 2000.

—. *The Unbearable Lightness of Being.* Trans. Henry Heim. Harper Perennial, 2009.

Lester, Richard. *Superman II.* Warner Bros., 1980.

Lewis, C.S. *The Abolition of Man.* HarperOne, 2015.

—. *Perelandra.* Scribner, 2003.

—. *The Screwtape Letters.* HarperOne, 2015.

Lindelof, Damon. *Watchmen.* HBO, 2019.

Lindsay, James A., and Mike Nanya. "Postmodern Religion and the Faith of Social Justice." *Areo.* 2018. Available online.

Linklater, Richard. *Waking Life.* Fox Searchlight Pictures, 2001.

Luhrmann, Baz. *Moulin Rouge!* 20th Century Fox, 2001.

Lycett, Andrew. *Dylan Thomas: A New Life.* Phoenix, 2004.

MacCulloch, Diarmiad. *Christianity: The First Three Thousand Years.* Penguin, 2011.

Mangold, James. *Logan.* 20th Century Fox, 2017.

Maritain, Jacques. *Dream of Descartes.* Trans. Mabelle L. Andison. Philosophical Library, 1944.

Martin, Michael. *Sophia in Exile*. Angelico Press, 2021.

Mayer, Lawrence S., and Paul R. McHugh. "Sexuality and Gender." *The New Atlantis*. 2016. Available online.

Max, D.T. *Every Love Story is a Ghost Story: A Life of David Foster Wallace*. Penguin, 2013.

McDonagh, John Michael. *Calvary*. Momentum Pictures, 2014.

McTeigue, James. *V for Vendetta*. Warner Bros. Pictures, 2006.

Mead, G.R.S., editor. *Pistis Sophia: A Gnostic Gospel*. Mockingbird, 2017.

Merton, Thomas. *Zen and the Birds of Appetite*. New Directions, 1968.

Miles, Jack. *God: A Biography*. Vintage, 1996.

Mill, John Stuart. *On Liberty*. Hackett, 1978.

Miller, Arthur. *The Crucible*. Penguin, 2003.

Miyamoto, Shigeru. *Super Mario World*. Nintendo, 1990.

Moonface. *City Wrecker*. Jagjaguwar, 2014.

— . *Dreamland EP: Marimba and Shit-Drums*. Jagjaguwar, 2010.

— . *Julia with Blue Jeans On*. Jagjaguwar, 2013.

— . *Organ Music Not Vibraphone Like I'd Hoped*. Jagjaguwar, 2011.

— . *This One's for the Dancer and This One's for the Dancer's Bouquet*. Jagjaguwar, 2018.

Morales, Vincent. *The Divine Secret of Nothing*. E-Book-Time, 2011.

Morson, Gary Saul. "How the Great Truth Dawned." *The New Criterion*. Available online.

Murakami, Haruki. *Men Without Women*. Trans. Philip Gabriel and Ted Goossen. Vintage, 2018.

Nichols, Sallie. *Jung and Tarot: An Archetypal Journey*. Samuel Weiser, 2004.

Nietzsche, Friedrich. *A Nietzsche Compendium*. Ed. David Taffel. Sterling Publishing, 2008.

O'Siadhail, Micheal. *The Five Quintets*. Canterbury Press, 2019.

Ovid. *Metamorphoses*. Trans. David Raeburn. Penguin, 2004.

Paglia, Camille. *Sexual Personae*. Vintage, 1991.

Palahniuk, Chuck. *Rant*. Anchor, 2008.

Paz, Octavio. *The Double Flame: Love and Eroticism*. Trans. Helen Lane. Harcourt, 1996.

—. *An Erotic Beyond: Sade*. Trans. Eliot Weinberger. Houghton Mifflin Harcourt, 1998.

—. *Five Works*. Trans. Helen Lane, Donald Gardner, and Rachel Phillips. Arcade Classics, 2012.

Percy, Walker. *The Last Gentleman*. Picador, 1999.

—. *Lost in the Cosmos*. Picador, 2000.

—. *The Second Coming*. Picador, 1980.

Peterson, Jordan B. *Maps of Meaning*. Taylor and Francis Books, 1999.

Phillips, Todd. *Joker*. Warner Bros. Pictures, 2019.

Pinker, Stephen. *Enlightenment Now*. Penguin, 2018.

Pizzolatto, Nic, and Cary Joji Fukunaga. *True Detective, Season 1*. United States: HBO, 2014.

Plato. *Five Dialogues: Euthyphro, Apology, Crito, Meno, Phaedo*. Trans. G.M.A. Grube. Hackett, 2002.

—. *The Republic*. Trans. G.M.A. Grube. Hackett, 1992.

—. *The Symposium*. Trans. Christopher Gill. Penguin, 2003.

Polikoff, Daniel Joseph. *In the Image of Orpheus: Rilke — A Soul History*. Chiron, 2011.

Postman, Neil. *Amusing Ourselves to Death*. Penguin, 2005.

Pullman, Philip. *The Good Man Jesus and the Scoundrel Christ*. Canongate Books, 2010.

—. *His Dark Materials*. Knopf, 2002.

Ragan, Chuck. *Exister*. Rise Records, 2012.

Rahner, Karl. *In Dialogue*. Crossroad Publishing, 1986.

Rank, Otto. *Art and Artist: Creative Urge and Personality Development*. W.W. Norton & Company, 1989.

Renan, Ernest. *The Life of Jesus*. Trans. Great Minds. Prometheus, 1991.

Ricoeur, Paul. *Freud and Philosophy*. Trans. Denis Savage. Yale University Press, 1977.

Saint-Exupéry, Antoine de. *The Little Prince*. Trans. Richard Howard. Mariner Books, 2000.

Scorsese, Martin. *The Last Temptation of Christ*. Adapted from Nikos Kazantzakis. Universal Pictures, 1988.

Shakespeare, William. *Othello*. Oxford University Press, 2008.

Shelley, Mary. *Frankenstein*. Oxford University Press, 2009.

Shelley, Percy Bysshe. *Selected Poems and Prose*. Penguin, 2017.

Shestov, Lev. *Potestas Clavium*. Trans. Bernard Martin. Ohio University Press, 1968.

Sigdell, Jan Erik. *Was Yahweh an Anunnaku?* 2011. Available online.

Solovyov, Vladimir. *The Meaning of Love*. Trans. Thomas R. Beyer, Jr. Lindisfarne Books, 1985.

Solzhenitsyn, Aleksandr. *The Gulag Archipelago: An Experiment in Literary Investigation*. Ed. Edward E. Ericson, Jr. Harper Perennial, 2007.

Sophocles. *Oedipus the King*. Oxford University Press, 2009.

Stern, Karl. *Flight from Woman*. Paragon House, 1998.

Stiller, Ben. *The Secret Life of Walter Mitty*. 20th Century Fox, 2013.

Taleb, Nassim Nicholas. *The Black Swan*. Random House, 2010.

Taylor, Charles. *A Secular Age*. Belknap Press, 2018.

Tolstoy, Leo. *Anna Karenina*. Trans. Richard Pevear and Larissa Volokhonsky. Penguin, 2004.

—. *The Death of Ivan Ilyich and Other Stories*. Trans. Richard Pevear and Larissa Volokhonsky. Vintage, 2010.

Thoreau, Henry David. *Civil Disobedience*. Dover, 1993.

Turner, Luke. *Metamodernist Manifesto*. 2011. Available online.

Unknown Friend. *Meditations on the Tarot: A Journey into Christian Hermeticism*. Trans. Robert Powell. Angelico Press, 2020.

Urantia Foundation. *The Urantia Book*. Urantia Foundation, 2011.

Vaneigem, Raoul. *The Revolution of Everyday Life*. Trans. Donald Nicholson-Smith. PM Press, 2012.

Vico, Giambattista. *New Science*. Penguin, 2000.

Vodolazkin, Eugene. *Laurus*. Oneworld Publications, 2016.

Voegelin, Eric. *The New Science of Politics*. University of Chicago Press, 1987.

Wachowski Brothers. *The Matrix*. Warner Bros., 1999.

Wallace, David Foster. *Infinite Jest*. Back Bay Books, 2006.

— . *A Supposedly Fun Thing I'll Never Do Again*. Back Bay Books, 1998.

Washington, George. "Resignation of Military Commission." *National Archives*. 1783. Available online.

Weil, Simone. *Waiting for God*. Harper Perennial, 2009.

Wenders, Wim. *Wings of Desire*. The Criterion Collection, 2009.

Wilde, Oscar. *The Picture of Dorian Gray*. Oxford University Press, 2008.

Yorke, Thom. "Fitter Happier." *OK Computer*. Capitol, 1997.

Zmirak, John Patrick, Jr. *Walker Percy's Return to the Feminine*. Dissertation for Louisiana State University, 1996.

www.ingramcontent.com/pod-product-compliance
Lightning Source LLC
Chambersburg PA
CBHW022018090426
42739CB00006BA/194